THE REAL JESUS

Disciple-making Series | Book 3

The Real Jesus | Book 3
© 2025 by Adam Grill, D.D.

Published by Family Church
10717 Adams St.
Holland, MI 49423

ISBN 979-8-9989436-2-1

All rights reserved. No part of this publication may be reproduced, stored in a retrieval system, or transmitted in any form or by any means—for example, electronic, photocopy, recording—without the prior written permission of the publisher.

Except where noted, Scripture quotations are taken from the Holy Bible: New International Version (NIV) 2015. All rights reserved.

Cover image: Jesus rescues lamb from cliff © Kevin Carden| stock.adobe.com
Cover and book design: Family Church

CONTENTS

INTRODUCTION 3
HOW TO USE THIS BOOK 4
CHAPTER 49 7
THE GOOD SAMARITAN
CHAPTER 50 12
WORKING FOR THE LORD VS RESTING WITH THE LORD
CHAPTER 51 16
JESUS TEACHES ON PRAYER
CHAPTER 52 26
SIX LEADERSHIP FUNDAMENTALS FROM JESUS
CHAPTER 53 34
WHAT IS GODLY FRUIT?
CHAPTER 54 42
WHAT DOES A REAL DISCIPLE OF JESUS LOOK LIKE?
CHAPTER 55 51
LOST & FOUND
CHAPTER 56 59
WHAT'S LOVE GOT TO DO WITH IT?
CHAPTER 57 65
THE BEST IS YET TO COME
CHAPTER 58 73
A WARNING, FORGIVENESS, & THANKFULNESS
CHAPTER 59 78
PRAYER, RIGHTEOUSNESS, & RICHES
CHAPTER 60 86
JESUS TEACHES ON DIVORCE
CHAPTER 61 94
THE KINGDOM OF GOD IS LIKE
CHAPTER 62 102
TRIUMPHAL ENTRY
CHAPTER 63 109
JESUS' SECOND CLEANSING OF THE TEMPLE

CHAPTER 64..........................115
JESUS PREDICTS HIS DEATH

CHAPTER 65..........................122
BUCKING AUTHORITY

CHAPTER 66..........................131
JESUS' VIEW OF TAXES & ETERNAL MARRIAGE

CHAPTER 67..........................138
THE GREATEST COMMANDMENT

CHAPTER 68..........................145
GREATEST COMMANDMENT PART II - A SELFLESS COMMAND

CHAPTER 69..........................152
LEARNING FROM HYPOCRITES

CHAPTER 70..........................160
JESUS ON END TIMES – PART 1

CHAPTER 71..........................167
JESUS ON END TIMES – PART 2

FROM PASTOR ADAM...............174
NEXT IN *THE REAL JESUS* SERIES
NOTES

INTRODUCTION

Welcome to the third book in *The Real Jesus* series! If you haven't read the prior two books, I suggest you pick up a copy and start with them. This series is a chronological walk-through of Jesus' life. This book begins at chapter 49 to remind you that it is a continuation of the story of Jesus' life.

Book 3 begins with the story of the Good Samaritan and Jesus' teachings on what it means to be a good neighbor. You will also read about Jesus' approach to life issues, such as how to pray, what leadership under Jesus looks like, what a real disciple of Jesus looks like, how the best is yet to come, and what Jesus' view is on divorce. You will even read about when Jesus got so MAD at people for not treating God's house (the temple) how they should have that He drove people out of the temple with a whip!

This book concludes with Jesus' teaching on what the **GREATEST** commandment is. You will hear Jesus say the **GREATEST** thing we can do is love God and love people. I hope that by now, you are using books 1 and 2 to teach others about Jesus. In doing that, you are living out your love for God and love for people. These books are not created solely to increase your knowledge of God, but to provide you with a simple tool to help you share the love of God.

Read with an open mind and heart. Jesus has so much for you to learn about His life and how to apply it to your life in today's ever-changing world. I hope that as you read these books, you will be transformed by learning more about God's love for us. It is a love so great that He sent His one and only Son to earth to teach us how life was designed to be lived and to become our pathway to eternal life with God.

HOW TO USE THIS BOOK

 READ & DISCUSS

I encourage you to read and discuss this book with another person or with a small group of people. This book was designed to be studied with one or more people because that was what Jesus modeled for us throughout His life here. This book is a simple tool to help anyone walk through Jesus' life chronologically and learn who the real Jesus was, is, and always will be.

 KEY PASSAGES

Each chapter has specific Bible passages to read. Let me encourage you to buy or download a copy of the Bible to read as we go on this journey together. All the passages quoted in this book are from the New International Version. I would also suggest buying a copy of Thomas & Gundry's *The NIV Harmony of the Gospels*, which pulls out all the Bible passages about Jesus' life and puts them in chronological order for you.

 READ

Read those passages in your Bible or *Harmony of the Gospels* before continuing with the book. You will also find parts of the Bible sprinkled throughout the book. Every time I directly quote the Bible, those words will be in *red italics.* This is done to help you distinguish God's Word from mine. You will also see that whenever God, Jesus, and the Holy Spirit are referenced (He, Him, They, Me, My, etc.), it will always begin with a capital letter because it helps remind us that we are referring to God, Jesus, or The Holy Spirit.

❓ WEEKLY DISCUSSION QUESTIONS

When you gather, I encourage you to begin EACH SESSION with the same three questions. We do this to help you get to know your disciples personally and to become aware of what is happening in their lives. Start with these questions every time:
- What is one thing you are most thankful for since we last met?
- What is one thing that stressed you out most since we last met?
- What did you do to follow through on your last "I will" statements?

LIFE APPLICATION

At the end of every chapter, there will be a Life Application section. There, you will find one question that is unique to each chapter and two questions that are the same. Honest answers are always best. The questions help generate conversation and help you consider how to apply Jesus' life to your daily life.

Discuss your answers to all three questions when you get together. I encourage you to write your disciple's "I will" statements in your book next to their names. That way, when you meet, you can ask them how they did at following up on their "I will" statement.

LEADING OTHERS

There are several ways to walk through this book with others, depending on how much your disciples want to read each week. The two methods we have seen work the best are:
- Read one chapter a week and meet weekly or bi-weekly. When you gather, start with prayer and the opening questions. Then,

talk through the highlights you and your disciples recall from the chapter. Next, have everyone share how they answered the Life Application questions. Pray together and schedule your next time to meet.

- Read one chapter daily and gather weekly or bi-weekly to discuss. When you gather, start with prayer and the opening questions. Then, talk through everyone's single big takeaway from each chapter read. Next, share how everyone answered the Life Application questions. Pray together and schedule your next time to meet.

CHAPTER 49

THE GOOD SAMARITAN

 Luke 10:25-37

Many religions believe in eternal life, although the afterlife looks vastly different in each of them. The process of attaining eternal life also varies according to each religion. So, how can someone know if there is such a thing as eternal life, and if there is, how can they attain it? That is the exact question posed in the Bible passage you are about to read.

 Luke 10:25-29

Let me give you a little context for this passage. The *²⁵ expert in the law* did not ask Jesus this question because he wanted to know the answer. This expert asked it because he thought he could trap Jesus with his brilliant question. His question is one that people still ponder to this day: *²⁵ "What must I do to inherit eternal life?"* Jesus, in His wisdom, turned the question back to the lawyer and asked him, *²⁶ "What is written in the Law?"* The lawyer answered correctly, quoting Deuteronomy 6:5 and Leviticus 19:18, saying, *²⁷ "'Love the Lord your God with all your heart and with all your soul and with all your strength and with all your mind; and, Love your neighbor as yourself.'"* Jesus affirmed His answer and said, *²⁸ "Do this and you will live."*

Do not forget where this chapter started. Is there such a thing as eternal life, and if there is, how do we attain it? Jesus affirmed the Jewish teaching that attaining eternal life comes through *²⁷ "Love the Lord your God with all your heart and with all your soul and with all your strength and with all your mind; and, Love your neighbor as yourself."* Jesus' answer begs the question: Do you love

God with ALL your heart, soul, strength, and mind? Do you love other people as much as you love yourself? If those are keys to eternal life, it is very important that you can answer yes without any doubts.

The lawyer, seeking to justify himself, came back at Jesus with another question. He asked, *²⁹ "And who is my neighbor?"* This question sets the stage for Jesus to tell the parable of the Good Samaritan.

It's important to know the teachers of the law were Jewish, and, at the time, Jewish people had a deep-seated animosity toward Samaritans. It began when Assyria conquered the northern kingdom of Israel in 722 B.C. The Assyrians resettled the Jewish lands with people who did not believe in God, and these foreigners brought their pagan idol worship with them. This led the Samaritans to blend the worship of God with the pagan idols. However, devoted Jewish people found that to be abhorrent because God said to never worship another god besides Him. To make matters worse, intermarriages also took place, which was against Jewish law. Furthermore, the Samaritans and Jewish people also had political and territorial disputes.

 Luke 10:30-37

In the parable, a man traveled from Jerusalem to Jericho, and robbers attacked him. They stripped him of his clothes, beat him, and left him half-dead. A priest, or a modern-day pastor like me, happened to go down the same road and saw the man beaten and bloody in the ditch. He responded like many would; he didn't want to get involved and passed by without helping. Then a Levite, like a modern-day worship leader, passed by and did the same thing. Then a Samaritan came to the same place, did the opposite of the first two, and helped this beaten-up man. The Samaritan went to the man, bandaged his wounds, put the man on his donkey, brought him to an inn, and cared for him. However, his kindness did not stop there! *³⁵ "The next day he took out two denarii and gave them to the innkeeper. 'Look after him,' he said, 'and when I return, I will reimburse you for any extra expense you may have.'"*

Can you imagine being that generous? Can you imagine helping a stranger like that? Let me give you additional context that makes this even more astounding. In Jesus' time, the value of two denarii was equivalent to about two days' wages for a common laborer. Would you give two full days' pay to help a random person on the street? Most people think they are generous if they offer a homeless person one hour's wage.

Jesus then asked the lawyer, *³⁶ "Which of these three do you think was a neighbor to the man who fell into the hands of robbers?" ³⁷ The expert in the law replied, "The one who had mercy on him."* Can you imagine how much it pained a Jewish man to admit that the Samaritan man was right in this situation? Then Jesus said, *³⁷ "Go and do likewise."* Jesus was telling a Jewish man the BEST thing he could do in life was to act like a Samaritan man. Can you imagine if God told you the BEST thing you can do in life is to act like a group of people you hate?

This parable is rich with lessons and applications for our lives today. Here are a few key points to consider:

True Neighborliness
The parable challenges us to expand our understanding of who our neighbor is. It is not limited to people like us or those we are comfortable with. Our neighbor includes anyone in need, regardless of race, religion, or social status. The Samaritan, whom the Jewish people despised, exemplifies true neighborliness by showing compassion and mercy to the injured man.

Compassion in Action

The Samaritan's actions demonstrate that genuine compassion involves more than feeling pity. It requires taking action to help those in need. Despite their religious status, the priest and the Levite failed to act out of compassion. On the other hand, the Samaritan went out of his way to care for the injured man, even at a significant personal cost.

Breaking Down Barriers

The parable also highlights the importance of breaking down social and cultural barriers. The animosity between Jews and Samaritans was well-known, yet the Samaritan did not let this prevent him from helping the injured man. In the same way, Jesus calls us to overcome our prejudices and extend love and compassion to all people.

Eternal Life and Good Works

While the lawyer's initial question was about inheriting eternal life, Jesus' response shows we do not earn eternal life through good works alone. Instead, it is about living out the love and compassion that God has shown us. Our good works reflect our faith and love for God. If we truly love God, even the people who are nothing like us will see a reflection of God in our actions.

The parable of the Good Samaritan calls us to love our neighbors as ourselves, show compassion in action, and break down barriers that divide us. It challenges us to live out our faith daily by demonstrating God's love for everyone.

 LIFE APPLICATION

- Think about the people you tend to avoid. How could you reach out and selflessly serve them in a way that could lead

them toward God?
- In today's reading, what did you learn about God, yourself, and mankind?
- As a result of today's reading, how will you apply what you learned? Answer as I will…

CHAPTER 50

WORKING FOR THE LORD VS RESTING WITH THE LORD

 Luke 10:38-42

I am a type A person. I am driven and love to work. Before I was a pastor, I worked in the construction industry, and my first job was a construction superintendent. The majority of my job was going from job site to job site, ensuring the trades were working hard and doing things to our company's standards. We did not tolerate people sitting around and doing nothing. Due to my type A personality and the way I am wired, it is hard for me to rest. In the passage you are about to read, you will learn how sometimes the best thing we can do is rest.

 Luke 10:38-42

Martha worked hard to prepare their home to serve Jesus well, the same thing many people do when guests come over. Just like my wife before the company arrives, she is always busy sweeping and mopping floors, picking up things, shifting furniture, cooking, and more. Everything my wife does, everything Martha did, comes from a good heart that wants to serve other people well and show them they are thought of.

Mary was so caught up by Jesus that she sat at his feet, talking or listening to Him. For many people, those who choose to act like Mary are looked at as lazy by Martha-types. I wish I could say that I am a Mary-type person when guests come over, but that would not be true.

What did Jesus mean when He said, *⁴¹ "Martha, Martha," the Lord answered, "you are worried and upset about many things,*

⁴² but few things are needed—or indeed only one. Mary has chosen what is better, and it will not be taken away from her." We can all understand that getting caught up and worrying about "many things" is not good for anyone. That being said, why is it that what Mary did was "better?"

The key point of this passage is the importance of prioritizing spiritual nourishment and spending time in the presence of the Lord over being consumed with worldly distractions. Choosing to spend time with God, do devotions, pray, fast, attend church, get involved with youth group, or go on mission trips is not as easy as it sounds. Most people today think they are regular attenders if they are in church once per month or more, but we all know that one out of four isn't a passing grade anywhere.

Jesus gently rebuked Martha. *⁴¹ "Martha, Martha,"* the Lord answered, *⁴¹ "you are worried and upset about many things, ⁴² but few things are needed—or indeed only one."* Do not miss the end of Jesus's words, *"indeed only one."* Spending time with Jesus is more important than anything else in life. Jesus wanted Martha to realize that, and He wants you to know that as well. The greatest thing you do in life will not be about the company you build, the games you win, the wealth you accumulate, or anything else. This was a key mental shift I had to make in my life that helped me to better understand this concept and enrich my relationship with Jesus.

In the prior chapter, people wanted to know if there was such a thing as eternal life and how to get there. Jesus said there is eternal life and that fully loving God and other people is essential to attaining it. Think about this…what is the ONLY thing that is a part of this life and eternal life? What is the only thing that carries forward into eternal life from a Biblical worldview? Our physical bodies decay. Our wealth is passed down or given away. Our buildings will eventually be torn down. What lasts eternally?

Our soul, our spirit, the essence of who we are is the only

thing on Earth that carries forward into eternity. That is why spending time with God is far more important than anything else. Jesus stresses the importance of loving other people as much as we love God because we should want those people to be with God in heaven for all of eternity. If spending time with God is so important, it makes sense as to why the devil will do everything he can to distract us away from it, to keep us too busy, or to shift our focus to lesser things.

This story encourages us to examine our priorities. Are we too consumed with life's busy tasks to make time for spiritual growth and reflection? It challenges us to balance our outward responsibilities with inner reflection and seek spiritual fulfillment as a cornerstone of a meaningful and purposeful life.

 LIFE APPLICATION

- How much time do you spend with God, praying, reading your Bible, or attending church? How can you carve out more time for God?
- In today's reading, what did you learn about God, yourself, and mankind?
- As a result of today's reading, how will you apply what you learned? Answer as I will…

CHAPTER 51

JESUS TEACHES ON PRAYER

 Luke 11:1-13 & Matthew 6:5-15

In the Jewish tradition, religious teachers are called rabbis. In ancient times, following a rabbi meant your entire life revolved around becoming like him. Your walked behind your rabbi and studied everything he did. A good student would literally become covered in the dust of the rabbi who was walking in front of them. As we continue in this study on the life of Jesus and dive deep into walking as He walked, my prayer is for you to be covered in His dust.

 Luke 11:1-13

For many of us, our prayer life consists of praying over meals and asking for wishes to be granted. Prayer is a critically important part of the Christian life, but if we are honest, many people are uncomfortable praying in front of others. This discomfort comes from hesitancy to believe we will "pray the right way." Even Jesus' closest followers wanted to learn how to pray like Him. This is why, *¹ when he finished, one of his disciples said to him, "Lord, teach us to pray, just as John taught his disciples."* Watching Jesus pray and discovering that John the Baptist had taught his disciples to pray sparked these men's desire to also learn how to pray.

Discomfort in praying generally stems from the fear of saying the wrong thing or not knowing what to say. The good news is that Jesus can teach us how to pray and give us that confidence in any situation. Prayer acknowledges that God alone is all-powerful and that we must depend on Him. Jesus responded to His follower's request by saying, *² "When you pray, say: "'Father, hallowed be your name, your kingdom come. ³ Give us each day our daily bread. ⁴*

Forgive us our sins, for we also forgive everyone who sins against us. And lead us not into temptation.'" Matthew recorded the same prayer with more detail.

 Matthew 6:5-15

In these teachings from Jesus, you can see that the words are not identical. This tells me that Jesus did not intend for us to repeat these words verbatim but rather to use them as a guide. This means it is normal for each of us to talk differently with God. Learning to pray is simply learning to speak with God. Jesus showed us that. Since we all communicate differently, how we talk to God will also be different. Quiet people of few words may pray short prayers that are to the point. People who love to speak may have long conversational prayers to God. Neither is better, but it's important to remember a few key points. Let's break down Jesus' prayer into parts to help us understand what is critical.

The prayer of Jesus began with, *⁹ "Our Father in heaven."* Therefore, the first crucial point is this:

When we pray, start with a proper view of God as Father.

Some people find it difficult to call God "Father" because it conjures up negative thoughts of their earthly father. If you had a great father, you will likely have no problem with this. If you had a non-existent or bad father, it may be more difficult because saying "Father" implies a close personal relationship. In the New Testament, Jesus called God "Father" more than 70 times.

Let me put this in perspective. When I am doing sermon prep, my office door is normally closed. I don't answer my phone calls, texts, or emails. I am focused. If one of my kids enters my office, I stop everything. I get a big smile on my face and greet them warmly. I do this because I love my kids, and I want them to know they can always come to me. I will always be their loving father, just like God is always there when we need Him. We always have access to a loving Father. **Do you see God as your loving Father who desires to converse with you?**

Calling someone a father also implies a level of respect and submission in the relationship. In our day, it seems that the reverse is true. Many American Christians treat God as their homie, friend, buddy in the sky, or genie in a bottle. We don't fear God. We don't fear making God angry. We don't pray for God's will. We pray and ask Him to do our will. We're too casual about God. The author of Hebrews 12:19 phrased it this way, *"Moreover, we have all had human fathers who disciplined us and we respected them for it. How much more should we submit to the Father of spirits and live!"* We must always do so when we approach God with reverence, respect, and submission to His sovereign authority.

Jesus doesn't stop there. Once He taught us to firmly place God as *"Our Father,"* He continued with *⁹ "Our Father in heaven, hallowed be your name."*

When we pray, continue by praising God.

I am sure some of you wonder what that even means. Hallowed is defined as "sanctified or consecrated." To say something is hallowed is to say you are setting it apart as holy, to be respected, honored, or revered. Hallowed refers to someone we have an awe and utmost respect for because they deserve it. It would be like treating someone better than you would a professional athlete or a famous person you idolize. Think of someone with whom you would be in awe if you met them; that is how Jesus said we are to approach God. He was telling us that the very name of God should be respected. We should never treat God's name with disrespect, as some do when they curse and use His name negatively. For example, OMG is one of the top texted abbreviations in today's culture. OMG is short for OH MY GOD, and it is not said, or written, to show reverence to God. It is taking the Lord's name in vain... breaking one of the Ten Commandments. We should give the same respect and honor to God's name that we offer to God because He and His name are one and the same. It is critical in our prayer life to put God in the proper place of respect, love, and submission to Him. Then, we can continue by praising God for who He is, not because of what He has done in our lives, but simply because He *is* the one true God.

Next, Jesus moves us deeper into our prayer: *9 "'Our Father in heaven, hallowed be your name, 10 your kingdom come, your will be done, on earth as it is in heaven.'"*

When we pray, we focus on the Father's kingdom.

Our prayer should not simply list our needs. There is nothing wrong with taking our needs to God, but our focus should not begin with our needs. Prayer isn't designed for our will to be done but for God's will to be done on earth. Therefore, our prayers should begin by focusing on two aspects of God's glory: His name to be revered and His kingdom to come. This was the constant focus of Jesus. What could this look like in your life?

If you are not a believer, pray for a desire to know Jesus, and pray for God's purpose to reign in your heart. If you are a believer, pray for the Great Commission to be at the forefront of all believers' minds. Pray for the church to set itself apart as holy. Pray that God's name will be glorified all over the earth, as people from every tongue, tribe, and nation come to bow before Him. If we approach God this way, it becomes natural for us to desire God's will in our lives. Pray that God's kingdom would come into the hearts of our family. Pray for others in the family of God. Pray that the church would live out God's purpose. Pray that the devil will be overthrown and that the rightful Lord of the universe will be enthroned as King. Pray for God to be glorified by His kingdom coming to our city, state, and nation. Pray for His kingdom to come around the world. Kingdom praying will affect your whole outlook on life. **Is this the first focus in your prayer life?**

When we pray, we focus on the Father's purpose, for His name to be glorified and for His kingdom to come. Only after this does Jesus mention our needs. *9 "'Our Father in heaven, hallowed be your name, 10 your kingdom come, your will be done, on earth as it is in heaven, 11 give us each day our daily bread.'"*

Jesus continues with three specific petitions.

When we pray, pray for our family's needs and provisions.

First, daily bread refers to our basic physical needs. It recalls the manna that God provided each day for Israel in the wilderness. God gave them enough to supply their need for that day, except on the day before the Sabbath, when they could gather enough for the following day. This reminds us that we are to live simply and depend on God and not trust in our resources.

Most of us have been blessed with far more than the necessities. We have plenty for weeks or months to come. Even though we have all we need, we dare not forget that it all can be taken away instantly. Jesus reminds us to remember that the reason we ask God for provision is not so that we can be happy, but so that we can experience His kingdom coming to us through His power of provision. **When was the last time you walked through your home and thanked God for a bed to sleep in, a blanket, heat or air conditioning, water, a shower, soap, toothpaste, clothing, coffee, breakfast, and safety?**

The second petition involves forgiveness. *9 "'Our Father in heaven, hallowed be your name, 10 your kingdom come, your will be done, on earth as it is in heaven, 11 give us each day our daily bread.*

[12] And forgive us our sins, as we also forgive everyone who sins against us.'"

Pray for our need for forgiveness and help us forgive others.

As bread is a basic need for our bodies, forgiveness is a basic need for our souls. We all have sinned (done wrong things); therefore, we must seek forgiveness daily so that we can come before God with a clear conscience.

Forgiveness can be challenging, but think about it this way. I am my father's son because I was born into his family. I'll always be his son, even if I wrong him. He and I can only enjoy a close relationship if I confess it and ask him to forgive me when I have done wrong to him. In the same way, we will drift away from our relationship with the heavenly Father if we are not sensitive to our sin by coming to Him daily for forgiveness.

God's forgiveness is granted based on His grace, not our works. Forgiveness is critical. Look at what Jesus said in Matthew 6:14-15, *[14] "For if you forgive other people when they sin against you, your heavenly Father will also forgive you. [15] But if you do not forgive others their sins, your Father will not forgive your sins."* The point is that if we can forgive others, then surely God, who is perfect, will forgive us when we ask. However, note the words of Jesus: **We must forgive, in order to be forgiven.** Is there someone you refuse to forgive? Please pause for a minute and ask yourself if there is someone whom you will not forgive?

Some people have been hurt badly by someone else. Part of being a pastor is proclaiming the truth, and the Bible says that to be forgiven, we must forgive. If you have said, I forgive this person, but in your heart, you know you have not, then you still hold the offense against them. You have not entirely submitted in your heart to forgiving them. When you look at the person who hurt you, it still causes you to be angry. When you look at the person who hurt you, it makes you bristle because you have not truly forgiven and moved on.

Please listen to what Jesus said: You will not be forgiven if you do not forgive. Don't go through life clinging to the pain of unforgiveness. Give it up to God and, trust me, your life will be so much better! Trust the truth of God's Word; life is better when you forgive. If you cannot forgive them, can you honestly pray, "Father, forgive my sins," while you refuse to forgive someone who has sinned against you? Don't just walk away from a strained relationship as if it doesn't matter. If you're bitter, you can't pray rightly until you choose to forgive. **Do you pray for those who are hurt and bitter, that they will forgive those who have wronged them?**

The final petition is *⁹"'Our Father in heaven, hallowed be your name, ¹⁰ your kingdom come, your will be done, on earth as it is in heaven, ¹¹ give us each day our daily bread. ¹² And forgive us our debts, as we also forgive our debtors. ¹³ And lead us not into temptation, but deliver us from the evil one.'"* This is difficult to interpret because James 1:13-14 tells us that God does not tempt anyone to sin, but that our lust tempts us. James 1:2 instructs us to count it all joy when we encounter various trials and temptations. Why would Jesus tell us to pray that God would not do what He will not do? Why should we pray that God would spare us from that which is for our good?

Jesus seems to be using the word in the sense of avoidance of temptation to sin. Jesus wants us to cultivate the attitude of fleeing from every situation where we might be tempted. The idea is that God will lead us into His ways of righteousness, where we will be kept from sin. Therefore, the prayer, *¹³ "And lead us not into temptation,"* acknowledges the weakness and sinfulness of our hearts. It is an admission that if God were to withdraw His gracious hand, we would fall into sin immediately. It is an attitude that flees temptation rather than one that sees how close to the brink we can come.

Here is another example that may help. During the Iranian hostage crisis in 1979, Greg Livingstone was asked to provide a "Missions Minute" at a large evangelical church. They only gave him one minute to speak, so he chose to ask them two questions. The first one was, "How many of you are praying for the 52 American hostages being held in Iran?" Four thousand hands went up. "Praise the Lord," he said. "Now, put your hands down and let me ask another question: How many of you are praying for the 42 million Iranians being held hostage to Islam?" Four hands went up. Livingstone said, "What are you guys—Americans first and Christians second? I thought this was a Bible-believing church!"

Pray for our need for protection from sins of omission and commission in our thoughts, deeds, and actions.

If we learn to pray as Jesus instructs us, we will focus on the Father's purpose, which is that His name be hallowed and His kingdom come in all the earth. We will focus on His family's needs for provision, forgiveness, and protection from sin, not so that the family will be cozy and happy, but so that the family will have what they need to carry out the Father's purpose.

Clay is a simple, ordinary thing, consisting of dust and water. Yet, clay has endless possibilities of what it can become. As you work with it, it is ever changing and conforms to your touch. Here is an interesting thing about clay: it can become dry, and it can become hard. Clay can appear to become set and unchangeable. Yet, did you know you can rehydrate clay? Take a clay pot and break it into pieces. Place those pieces in water, and they will be moldable again.

We are like clay. We are ordinary people, but in the hands of God, there are endless possibilities for what we can become. If we become covered in the dust of Jesus, we can do anything! Jesus said that through Him, we can do EVEN GREATER things than He did (John 14:12). You may have been running from God for a long time, or you may feel broken and don't know if you can ever be put back together. It does not matter where you have been before today or how you have messed up in life. If you place yourselves in God's hands, He will rehydrate you. Then He can remold you into someone greater than you could ever imagine. Prayer can be your first step in that direction. Think about it, then pray.

 LIFE APPLICATION

- Read The Lord's Prayer every day this week and practice praying like that after reading it.
- In today's reading, what did you learn about God, yourself, and mankind?
- As a result of today's reading, how will you apply what you learned? Answer as I will…

CHAPTER 52

SIX LEADERSHIP FUNDAMENTALS FROM JESUS

 Luke 12:1-59

I have not always been a pastor. I grew up going to church, but honestly, my memories of church as a kid are not great. I remember my parents making me dress up, having to sit quietly, and being ridiculously bored the whole time.

We moved to Fowlerville, Michigan right before my 6th-grade year. We became a part of an amazing church called Fowlerville United Brethren in Christ, where I liked going. Then, the Christian college I attended forced us to go to chapel as a part of our weekly routine. After graduating from college, my wife and I moved to Ohio. I started my career in construction, and she started her career in teaching. For the first time in our lives, we were on our own and had to decide if we would go to church. We began church shopping, and it was hard finding a church that we both liked.

As my career took off and we started moving all over the country, we found ourselves church shopping quite often. Honestly, there were times when I had ZERO desire to go to church. There were seasons when I cared more about my career than I did about my relationship with God. Maybe you are feeling that way right now. Looking back, I thank God for all those experiences because they prepared me for where I am today.

One of the fastest-growing demographics at the church I lead is the de-churched. De-churched people are people who once attended a church but stopped for some reason. Some people went to church, but then it became irrelevant to them. Others had new things come into their lives that became a higher priority. Others had someone inside the church say or do something that hurt them. Some moved and never connected with a new church.

I have been in all of those camps at one point.

Now, I live in West Michigan—an area known for its church culture. It is assumed that most people attend church. However, studies have revealed that on any given Sunday, more people are NOT in church than ARE in church. There is a problem, a disconnect, or a misconception regarding being intricately connected to the church. This problem extends far beyond West Michigan and is the reality for the majority of the United States.

Jesus was in the leadership development phase of His ministry by this point. Jesus clearly taught His followers that they needed to lead very differently from the way of the religious leaders (Pharisees and Sadducees). Jesus continually drew a sharp distinction between the type of leaders He expected His disciples to be and the leaders of His time. Jesus clarified that He wanted His disciples to model a different way of life. These distinctions would have been a stark contrast to what these young men had grown up with. Jesus consistently stopped to point out how the leaders of Israel led. He then used Scripture to show the disconnect between their teaching and God's Word. In the following passage, Jesus stopped to teach some critical leadership principles.

 Luke 12:1-12

Listen to the words of Jesus: *¹ Meanwhile, when a crowd of many thousands had gathered, so that they were trampling on one another, Jesus began to speak first to his disciples, saying: "Be on your guard against the yeast of the Pharisees, which is hypocrisy. ² There is nothing concealed that will not be disclosed, or hidden that will not be made known. ³ What you have said in the dark will be heard in the daylight, and what you have whispered in the ear in the inner rooms will be proclaimed from the roofs."* Clearly, something the Jewish leaders were doing was wrong and something to be wary of or avoid. Jesus said their hypocrisy was a major problem. The leaders were saying one thing but living very differently. This is why Jesus said, *[1] "Be on your guard against the yeast of the Pharisees?"*

This provided a mental image that everyone in His time would have understood. He was describing how yeast worked. Putting a small amount of yeast in bread or wine makes a substantial change in a short period of time. It changes the whole batch and cannot be undone once it has entered the mix. A Jewish ritual for Passover was to throw away any yeast in your home during that season. This tradition was strictly followed by Jewish people going back to the time of the Exodus (over 1,500 years).

Jesus used this common practice in the Jewish community to teach His young leaders a critical element of leadership. He taught them that there were two types of yeast, and everyone needed to make sure they never internalized one kind because it would change them in a negative way. Jesus was telling them that they needed to stay away from the teachings and methods of the Pharisees and Sadducees because they were hypocrites. Here is the point. **Leaders who follow Jesus practice what they preach.**

Unfortunately, we still fall short with this today. The mission at the church I lead is to teach people how to love God, love people, and make disciples of Jesus. Most true Christians would agree that it is a great mission statement. Most true Christian people love the Great Commission. Yet few are actively discipling one other person to become more like Jesus (which is why I wrote these books—to help you be able to do that in a simple way). If we want to say we are for the Great Commission, we must do what it says. It is not called the "Great Omission," yet far too many still think that making disciples is the pastor's job.

I have heard many reasons why people don't feel comfortable trying to disciple others: "'I don't know the Bible well enough"; "I don't have time"; "I don't know where to start"; "church says it is the pastor's job, so I don't have to.'" Yet, Jesus said discipling others is a key to leadership in His kingdom. He calls us to beware of a lifestyle that demonstrates something other than what you say you believe. The problem with the Jewish religious leaders was that they were more interested in being right in their own eyes. They had somehow forgotten their job was to promote God's Truth.

The second point Jesus made to His young leaders: **Leaders of Jesus remain teachable and open to being transformed by Truth.**

Often, as we grow older, it gets harder to remain teachable. We think we know more than young people. It becomes harder to be transformed because change becomes more difficult. We like things just the way they are or and are comfortable in our routines. Jesus taught His leaders to continually learn and be transformed into a greater image of Him. I would caution you to never get to the point where you think you know or have seen it all. Do not put God in a box. Get rid of pride! Humble yourself before God! Here is why: *⁴ "I tell you, my friends, do not be afraid of those who kill the body and after that can do no more. ⁵ But I will show you whom you should fear: Fear him who, after your body has been killed, has authority to throw you into hell. Yes, I tell you, fear him."* This is a complex reality. We tend to fear things right in front of us. Jesus said, "Do not fear the temporary. Fear the God who has dominion over you for all of eternity."

Jesus also gave a clear warning: *⁸ "I tell you, whoever publicly acknowledges me before others, the Son of Man will also acknowledge before the angels of God. ⁹ But whoever disowns me before others will be disowned before the angels of God. ¹⁰ And everyone who speaks a word against the Son of Man will be forgiven, but anyone who blasphemes against the Holy Spirit will not be forgiven."* We cannot be afraid to acknowledge Him publicly! We cannot be afraid to tell our friends, family, co-workers, boss, or business partners about Jesus. **Leaders in Jesus' kingdom are not afraid to tell others about Him.**

 Luke 12:13-21

¹⁵ Then he said to them, "Watch out! Be on your guard against all kinds of greed; life does not consist in an abundance of possessions." Jesus reminded them and us not to be greedy. Life is much more than accumulating stuff, including money. It is not bad when your "land produces plentifully" (verse 16). It is not a bad thing when your business prospers. It is not bad to receive a promotion with a pay increase. It is not bad when your investments increase in value. None of that is the evil in this parable.

This man is not called a fool for being a productive farmer. God knows this world needs productive farmers and profitable businesses. The man is called a fool because of the way he used the increase in his riches. There is no indication of him being rich toward God. He kept building bigger barns and focusing on kicking back and living "the good life." In other words, his treasure was relaxing, eating, drinking, and having fun. That was his treasured life. The riches in his barns made it possible.

Verse 21 continues this difficult teaching. This is especially hard to comprehend in a developed country where we continually store up for self-serving reasons. We strive to get ahead of the pack. It is a "dog-eat-dog" world. We look forward to an easy retirement. It seems logical to tithe (give God 10% of our income) only after we have enough for ourselves. We offer up money for missions once we have enough saved for ourselves. Too often, we place God on the back burner of our lives until we have "enough" to feel secure. *²¹ "This is how it will be with whoever stores up things for themselves but is not rich toward God."*

Jesus often taught about money because money is directly tied to our hearts. The key here is important. Jesus was not saying we cannot have savings, even abundant savings. He was not saying we cannot have nice things. Instead, Jesus was saying that we cannot hoard everything we have for ourselves. We must value God more than any amount of money, possessions, or earthly security.

What was wrong was this man's way of handling his riches. God wants us to enjoy what He gives us. Yet even more than that, God wants us to use what He gives us to build His Kingdom and not hoard it for our pleasure.

 Luke 12:22-48

²² Then Jesus said to his disciples: "Therefore I tell you, do not worry about your life, what you will eat; or about your body, what you will wear. ²³ For life is more than food, and the body more than clothes." We live in a world filled with things to worry about. Simply saying, "stop worrying," does nothing to stop it.

A question to consider when you worry might be: **What are you really saying to God when you are overcome with worry?** Worry conveys to God a lack of belief.

Do you believe He can, will or is powerful enough, to provide for your needs in the difficult moments? Trusting God with everything is a disciple's path.

Jesus taught that worry would not keep them on the path He needed them on. **Jesus' leaders trust God in all things and do not worry.**

The second half of this passage taught us that we will not be caught off guard when focused. When we are focused, we look forward to what is coming. Focusing keeps us from worrying or being distracted by things around us. Jesus wants us to focus on what really matters because this life is not a game. This life is the foundation of the life to come. The things you do in this life will have eternal ramifications for you… good or bad. Jesus does not want His leaders to get distracted by the teachings of the world, no matter how good or enticing they sound.

That was part of the problem in this story. People were listening to the Pharisees and Sadducees because they liked their message. In the same way, we can be attracted to particular messages today: Messages that say there is no such thing as sin or hell, that everyone goes to heaven, or that love is everything. False teachings can distract us because they sound good. Do you think that may have been why Jesus started by saying to be careful what teachings you listen to? Do you think that may have been why Jesus ended this message by saying to stay focused because it is easy to get off course? Please take the advice we received from Jesus. Be careful to whom you listen, and remain focused on God's Word alone. **Jesus' leaders stay focused.**

LIFE APPLICATION

- False belief or teaching, pride, hypocrisy, or faulty focus can change your entire life. Do you have some house (heart) cleaning to do?
- In today's reading, what did you learn about God, yourself, and mankind?
- As a result of today's reading, how will you apply what you learned? Answer as I will…

CHAPTER 53

WHAT IS GODLY FRUIT?

 Luke 13

When my family moved from Florida to Virginia, I bought a banana tree and an orange tree to take with me. As I mentioned in Book One of *The Real Jesus*, I am not the best gardener. I knew Virginia would be too cold to keep the trees outside in the winter. I researched and discovered that I could move the trees inside and that they could survive with the help of special lights and fertilizers. I put both trees in my office at church and was excited when I saw my orange tree start to produce… bananas! I am kidding, of course; we all know that is impossible. Never in the history of the world has something produced something that it's not designed for. In today's passage, Jesus will touch on that reality and remind us of the kind of fruit we should be producing. However, before He gets to the spiritual fruit, Jesus reminds us of some difficult truths.

 Luke 13:1-5

¹ Now there were some present at that time who told Jesus about the Galileans whose blood Pilate had mixed with their sacrifices. ² Jesus answered, "Do you think that these Galileans were worse sinners than all the other Galileans because they suffered this way? ³ I tell you, no! But unless you repent, you too will all perish. ⁴ Or those eighteen who died when the tower in Siloam fell on them—do you think they were more guilty than all the others living in Jerusalem? ⁵ I tell you, no! But unless you repent, you too will all perish." Jesus mentioned two disasters that were well-known at that time. One was the evil actions of a man named Pilate. The other was a natural disaster. I have heard people say they cannot accept how God allows a horrible person to have money, happiness, and friends while a good person is poor, miserable, and friendless. If we are honest, we can all wonder why God allows terrible things to happen to good people. Jesus made the point that the Galileans were not more or less guilty than others. All are guilty of sin. Jesus said that **unless we repent, we will all perish.**

This is hard to teach and understand, especially when it happens to you. At the time I wrote this, my dad, who has always been a faithful follower of God, was diagnosed with cancer. The news was devastating because I could not imagine life without my father. It was hard not to succumb to the common questions people ask when things like this occur to the best of people. We want to scream, "Why, God?" The truth is that we live on a fallen and sin-filled planet, and bad things do happen to good and bad people alike. In Matthew 5:45, we read a hard truth. *[45] He causes his sun to rise on the evil and the good, and sends rain on the righteous and the unrighteous.*

We must remember that repentance is deciding to do something about your sin issues. We all have different things we struggle with when it comes to sin. Some struggle with gossiping, others struggle with lust, others struggle with greed, and so on. Repentance means we learn that God defines it as wrong and we make a concerted effort to overcome that struggle in our lives. It means asking Jesus to forgive us for it, and it also means we must change the direction of our life. We actively stop doing what we know we should not do.

Perishing means more than dying. It means being eternally separated from God with no second chance. We must ensure our heart is right before God because we never know when our time on Earth will be over. There is only one thing I can promise every person reading this: we will die at some point and stand before our Creator. The question is, **have you repented and given your life to Jesus before that or not?**

Jesus used these two examples of times when none of these people expected to die in order to make the point: **We must be ready by ensuring we are right with God!**

 Luke 13:6-9

After the warning *⁵ "unless you repent you will perish,"* Jesus used this parable to illustrate principles of God's judgment. *⁶ "A man had a fig tree growing in his vineyard, and he went to look for fruit on it but did not find any. ⁷ So he said to the man who took care of the vineyard, 'For three years now I've been coming to look for fruit on this fig tree and haven't found any. Cut it down! Why should it use up the soil?' ⁸ "'Sir,' the man replied, 'leave it alone for one more year, and I'll dig around it and fertilize it. ⁹ If it bears fruit next year, fine! If not, then cut it down.'"*

The man who owned this vineyard came seeking fruit. The first point is simple: **God looks for fruit in and from your life.** The fruit of our lives shows the kind of people we truly are. An apple tree will bring forth apples, not watermelons. A cow gives birth to another cow, not a deer. If Jesus Christ has truly touched your life, it will show in the fruit you bear. It will take time for the fruit to come forth. **What is the fruit God is looking for from you?**

The illustration should either cause us concern or give us hope. For three years, the owner of the vineyard (illustrating God) came seeking fruit. Again, he was looking for fruit, but there was no fruit. Therefore, he said to cut it down. The owner in the parable illustrated the patience of God in judgment. He waited for three years, and, even though the tree still bore no fruit, He gave it one more chance.

The farmer (illustrating Jesus) did not leave the tree alone. What did he do? He gave the tree (illustrating us) exceptional care. Here is something that should make you smile: Sometimes God's particular kind of care might make you feel like you have been abandoned in the trash pile because you are surrounded by manure. Farmers know that while manure might smell, be a bit sloppy, and seem like a mess, the manure makes all the difference. God might be nourishing and preparing you for the fruit that is yet to come but in a way you do not understand. We must trust God even when it does not make sense. God has given each of us many second chances. **What fruit of God do you see in your life? What can you point to in your life that could prove to Jesus you are His disciple?**

To help us, God listed some fruit of the Spirit in Galatians 5:22-23: *love, joy, peace, forbearance, kindness, goodness, faithfulness, gentleness, and self-control.* If you are a follower of Jesus, these words should describe your life—and you. Would anyone use these words to describe you? Perhaps God is letting you know He is looking for fruit from you because you know there isn't much or even any. Jesus may be asking you to come let Him work in your life and build into you these traits of a life lived for God.

Now look ahead to verses 18-21: *[18] Then Jesus asked, "What is the kingdom of God like? What shall I compare it to? [19] It is like a mustard seed, which a man took and planted in his garden. It grew and became a tree, and the birds perched in its branches." [20] Again he asked, "What shall I compare the kingdom of God to? [21] It is like yeast that a woman took and mixed into about sixty pounds of flour until it worked all through the dough."*

This was not the only time Jesus talked about mustard trees. So, what are they? There is a Mediterranean mustard "tree" named black mustard. It is an invasive plant that will consume the whole countryside quickly. It grows up to 15 feet tall, but one of its unique characteristics is that these 15-foot plants grow tightly together. They create an unsurpassable thicket that becomes a home to many species of birds, insects, and rodents. It becomes its own ecosystem!

Black mustard has landed in the United States. San Diego County has been invaded by it. It covers the hills with its brilliant yellow flowers, and along the way, it takes out the indigenous plants by releasing chemicals that stunt other plants' ability to thrive. This plant is so hearty and invasive that the United States government has set up an agricultural program to counter its effects. Why does all that matter? It matters because Jesus said His kingdom will be like that.

When we transplant into a new area, we should forever change that landscape. We should stunt the growth of bad things and promote the growth of good things. This ties to the whole idea of being yeast as well. Yeast completely changes what it is mixed into. Here is the point: **Followers of Jesus should transform their environment to be more like heaven!** Followers of Jesus are not here to just coast through life and look like everyone else. We should change the people around us. We should change our schools, our communities, our states, our nation, and our world.

 Luke 13:22-27

Don't miss this! Heaven is found through a narrow door. Jesus says make every effort to get to heaven because many will try and yet they will not make it there. That should concern us. Really look at what Jesus said: *²⁴ "Make every effort to enter through the narrow door, because many, I tell you, will try to enter and will not be able to. ²⁵ Once the owner of the house gets up and closes the door, you will stand outside knocking and pleading, 'Sir, open the door for us.' "But he will answer, 'I don't know you or where you come from.' ²⁶ "Then you will say, 'We ate and drank with you, and you taught in our streets.' ²⁷ "But he will reply, 'I don't know you or where you come from. Away from me, all you evildoers!'"* There are going to be people who clearly think they are destined for heaven, only to discover they are not. This group of people will say: "Jesus, we went to church, we taught Sunday School, we were in a small group, we even went on a mission trip! Jesus, we know who You are!" The truth is that knowing who someone is does not mean you truly know them.

My goal as a pastor is to make sure that I help as many people as possible never hear those terrifying words said to them. Strive to enter through the narrow door. This is not a call to save yourself by good works. Good works do not lead to the narrow door. You may strive to enter throughout your lifetime but if you are not striving for the right door, it won't matter. Here is the point: **Jesus is the gate; He is the door. Entrance into His home requires a personal relationship with Jesus.**

There are many obstacles in the way to us reaching the narrow door of heaven. The *world* is an obstacle. The *devil* is an obstacle. The worst obstacle is probably our *minds*. Our *money* can be as well and so can all the *distractions* that keep us from spending time with God.

Do you realize that this life is not a game and that it has eternal ramifications? Every person will find themselves standing before God, weeping, pleading, rationalizing, but it will be too late. God is generous. He waits for us. He is patient with us. He gives us a second, third, fourth, and so many more chances. However, our time is finite, and if we do not find a relationship with Jesus before our time runs out, we will be eternally separated from God. Are you sure of your eternal destiny? **If you stood before Jesus today, what fruit could you show to prove you are His?**

 **LIFE APPLICATION**

- Imagine today was your last day. You wake up, and before you stands Jesus. What could you show if He asked you to show Him the fruit of your life produced for Him? What would you say? Write that down. If you cannot think of anything, today is the day to begin living a life that is all about building God's Kingdom.
- In today's reading, what did you learn about God, yourself, and mankind?
- As a result of today's reading, how will you apply what you learned? Answer as I will…

CHAPTER 54

WHAT DOES A REAL DISCIPLE OF JESUS LOOK LIKE?

 Luke 14

I grew up going to church, but I do not think I ever heard a sermon on what it looks like to be a disciple of Jesus. Or if I did, it did not keep my attention long enough to remember later on. I went to seminary. We studied the Bible and talked about how to do ministry, but we never defined what a disciple was. After I had been in ministry for a few years, I found myself at a conference that focused on Jesus. While there, I was asked to define what a disciple of Jesus was and what a real, authentic disciple of Jesus looked like. In this passage, we will find some of those characteristics, and they may not be what you expect.

 Luke 14:1-6

¹ One Sabbath, when Jesus went to eat in the house of a prominent Pharisee, he was being carefully watched. Jesus loved to gather around meals. Jesus knew eating together opened conversation, and He used mealtime to organically teach even those who hated Him the truth of what it means to be His disciple. Jesus used mealtime purposefully, and you can as well.

Can I suggest making it a priority to eat dinner around a table without technology? Ask those you eat with what brought them joy or frustration in their day. This simple conversation can help others make the connection between what is going on in their life and the work of God around them.

The importance of mealtimes has been studied, and research shows that families who eat together are more connected and fight less. Invite others to join you at mealtime, and if you live alone, make it a priority to invite someone to your table once a week to share a meal and have a purposeful conversation. As a normal part of mealtimes, I begin by asking purpose-filled questions of everyone at the table. This is a simple way to begin the discipling process with your family, friends, and neighbors!

In the Ten Commandments, God instructed us to keep the Sabbath holy and as a day of rest from our labors. For Christians, the Sabbath is on Sunday. In Jesus' time, it was deemed wrong to do any type of work on the Sabbath. People completed most cooking before the Sabbath began so that they didn't violate God's commandment. Some of you may have been raised in a tradition that followed this, even refusing to allow children to play on Sunday.

In this passage, Jesus healed a man on the Sabbath, and Jesus knew the Pharisees would consider this gesture to be work. Jesus continued breaking the religious traditions and instead focused more on the profound truths of His Father. He focused on God's will versus religious rules and on building God's Kingdom instead of upholding religious traditions. Jesus was teaching another discipleship principle: **Keep the Sabbath holy and restful, but enjoy your rest and invite others into your rest. Minister to those in need, share a meal, visit a sick friend, pray, and even heal another person's wounds.**

Jesus called out the religious leaders for acting in a way that was hypocritical. These leaders were angry with Jesus for healing on the Sabbath. Yet, these same religious leaders found it acceptable to help a stranded animal on the Sabbath. These religious people had been watching Jesus closely, hoping to catch Him doing something against their rules. If they succeeded, they hoped to discredit Jesus or, if possible, have Him arrested and be rid of Him for good. However, Jesus's example in this passage exposed how their theology was wrong. That is why they clammed up and said nothing. Their silence gave Jesus an open window to dive headfirst into a more profound teaching.

 Luke 14:7-14

This story about meals and honor was an unusual parable because it was abundantly clear to whom Jesus was referring. In this first parable, Jesus emphasized the selection of seats of honor. In the next parable, Jesus talked about the invitation list. Bear in mind that Jesus lived in an honor and shame culture, which meant that avoiding shame and receiving honor was of the utmost importance. If you or a family member did something wrong, public shame had tangible implications. Public shame would affect whom you could marry, the price you paid at the market, and who would be seen with you.

Jesus used this story to give us another practical trait of a true disciple. *⁸"When someone invites you to a wedding feast, do not take the place of honor, for a person more distinguished than you may have been invited. ⁹If so, the host who invited both of you will come and say to you, 'Give this person your seat.' Then, humiliated, you will have to take the least important place. ¹⁰But when you are invited, take the lowest place, so that when your host comes, he will say to you, 'Friend, move up to a better place.' Then you will be honored in the presence of all the other guests."*

At this point, you might conclude this was a lesson on how to look good at your next event, but looking better was not the point. *¹¹"For all those who exalt themselves will be humbled, and those who humble themselves will be exalted."* Jesus teaches that this life is not about status, honor, or a seat at the right table. Life is about humility and placing Jesus in the proper seat of honor. The lesson for us is this: **A true disciple is humble.**

Is being humble easy? Truthfully, not for everyone. It can be difficult for those with strong personalities and for extremely successful people. Just because you are wired not to be humble does not mean you get a free pass to act as you please. If you are a disciple of Jesus, you look at things differently. You know it isn't about you; it is about something far bigger than you.

Jesus continued with this: *¹² Then Jesus said to his host, "When you give a luncheon or dinner, do not invite your friends, your brothers or sisters, your relatives, or your rich neighbors; if you do, they may invite you back and so you will be repaid. ¹³ But when you give a banquet, invite the poor, the crippled, the lame, the blind, ¹⁴ and you will be blessed. Although they cannot repay you, you will be repaid at the resurrection of the righteous."* Jesus talked often about how, at the end of our lives, we will be rewarded in heaven based on what we did in this life. This also means we will not be rewarded if we do nothing. Jesus modeled humility and told us to be humble. Humility will be rewarded. Serve people whom others would never serve; invite the unloved to your table. Jesus invites sinners and saints to His table, saints who will lead sinners closer to Him. One great question to ask yourself is: **Who could you invite to your table and into your life? A true disciple serves those who are overlooked.**

 Luke 14:16-24

¹⁶ Jesus replied: "A certain man was preparing a great banquet and invited many guests. ¹⁷ At the time of the banquet he sent his servant to tell those who had been invited, 'Come, for everything is now ready.' ¹⁸ "But they all alike began to make excuses. The first said, 'I have just bought a field, and I must go and see it. Please excuse me.' ¹⁹ "Another said, 'I have just bought five yoke of oxen, and I'm on my way to try them out. Please excuse me.' ²⁰ "Still another said, 'I just got married, so I can't come.' ²¹ "The servant came back and reported

this to his master. Then the owner of the house became angry and ordered his servant, 'Go out quickly into the streets and alleys of the town and bring in the poor, the crippled, the blind and the lame.'"

There was nothing inherently wrong with what these people were doing. Those were all fine reasons for not being able to attend a party. We must remember Jesus told parables that dug deep into the motives of those He was talking to. Jesus looked into the heart and He knew the justifications and excuses for why they could not go. Remember that whenever Jesus was talking, there was always a deeper spiritual meaning to what He was talking about.

At this point, Jesus had been ministering for around three years, which means we are reading about things that happened during His final year of ministry. Jesus, just like His disciples, went first to reach God's chosen people (the Jewish people) with the Good News of His coming to build the Kingdom of God. Despite their efforts, far too many of the Jewish people chose not to believe in Jesus. They did not believe in Him because He did not uphold their early religious rules and practices. Jesus asked them to do things they did not want to do, and they chose not do them because doing so would come with a high personal cost. It was too much. They had excuses for not following Jesus. They used those same excuses to explain why they refused their invitation to the banquet He was preparing, otherwise known as eternal life!

Let's take a minute and talk about "reasons" versus "excuses." All the reasons these people chose for not following Jesus were not bad; they were busy and had things to do. Their answer may have been "next year when things settle down" or "when I have time to give the proper attention." Honestly, the reasons why you choose not to follow Jesus fully are not necessarily bad. But here is the rub: there is nothing wrong with retirement in Florida unless Jesus called you to be in ministry in the Upper Peninsula of Michigan. There is nothing wrong with having your kids in sports unless that means you never go to church because of games on Sunday morning. There is nothing wrong with wanting to get married unless your spouse does not care for God, and it causes you to wander away from the faith. There is nothing wrong with most things unless they become excuses that affect your ability to listen to and follow Jesus. The point is that following Jesus always come at a cost. **A true disciple does not make excuses; they make disciples.**

²² "'Sir,' the servant said, 'what you ordered has been done, but there is still room.' ²³ "Then the master told his servant, 'Go out to the roads and country lanes and compel them to come in, so that my house will be full. ²⁴ I tell you, not one of those who were invited will get a taste of my banquet.'" Most people would say they would like to go to heaven, which is a place they refer to as an eternal banquet in the sky. I would venture to say that most people would shudder at the thought of this life ending and them standing before Jesus with nothing but excuses. How would you answer Jesus as He looks straight into your eyes, asking why you never did any of the things He asked of you? Do not miss what Jesus said in this passage: those who do not become humble, those who refuse to care for society's outcasts, will be excluded from the final banquet. **Cost counting is critical.**

First-century culture relied on a particular way of life. Inviting friends, family, and rich neighbors was an appropriate tactic to secure one's place in that system. Reciprocal requests would ensue. Public acknowledgment of those social connections would come out. Rewards for following the rules of that system would follow. Jesus called into question that type of system, emphasizing the importance of hosts who chose to associate with people who were poor, crippled, lame, and blind. The problem for hosts, however, as Jesus explicitly recognized, was that no honor would come from those party guests. The point was and is: **A true disciple invests in the future kingdom.**

True disciples realize life is not about the here and now; it is about the Kingdom to come. True disciples understand they are investing in the future and desiring the reward in heaven, where it will be far richer and more meaningful than on earth. Heaven is where rewards are eternal. This was one of the key mental shifts that helped me follow God's call on my life to go into ministry. All good investors know you have to play the long game. I decided to play the long game spiritually and forgo some of the worldly pleasures and earthly treasures that do not last in favor of building God's Kingdom and striving for eternal rewards from God in heaven.

 Luke 14:26-35

This passage is intense. Remember, Jesus was not talking about what it seemed like on the surface. There was a deeper meaning. Do not take this literally. Jesus does not want you to hate the people you love most in life. Jesus was teaching about priorities. God does not want to be second fiddle to anyone or anything. God does not want to come after your spouse or your sports. God does not want you to tip him like you do a waiter. Jesus does not want you to live your life for yourself and then give Him the last couple of years after you have retired and can no longer travel. **Jesus wants the best of who we are, not the leftovers.**

This was His call to abandon the past and reset priorities based on Him. We must count the full cost because **a true disciple reorients their life around Jesus' mission.** Jesus ended His teaching with these words: *35 "Whoever has ears let them hear."* At this point, Jesus had been with many of these people for around three years, and guess what? They were listening, but they were not actively hearing Him. They were doing what you may do, what my kids do: letting things go in one ear and out the other. Jesus was, and still is, looking for people to put what He says into practice. He is not interested in us simply giving His teachings a nod and then returning to our preferred lifestyle.

 LIFE APPLICATION

- Have you ever weighed the cost of being Jesus' disciple? Are you prepared to give up anything He asks of you? Are you prepared to go anywhere He calls you to go? Are you willing to do anything He calls you to do? Ponder the limits on the cost of how far you will follow Jesus.
- In today's reading, what did you learn about God, yourself, and mankind?
- As a result of today's reading, how will you apply what you learned? Answer as I will…

CHAPTER 55

LOST & FOUND

 Luke 15

When I was a young boy, we lived in Frankenmuth, Michigan. If you have never been, you need to go. Frakenmuth is the home of Bronner's, the world's largest Christmas store. Frankenmuth is also famous for some of the best German food you can find outside of Germany. When we lived there, we had two big dogs that I loved. Unfortunately, when my dad was promoted, we had to move. My parents decided to build a house, meaning we would be living with family for an extended period.

Our family did not favor our big dogs living with them. Consequently, we had to give them away. However, a week before we moved, our neighbor (a farmer who took our dogs) called to say they had run away. I was distraught that my dogs were now lost. I pleaded with my dad to let me look for them, so we did. I will never forget them running out of the woods when they heard our voices calling for them. They were lost and then they were found! The joy of seeing my dogs alive and well will always be in my memory. In our passage today, we will see similar roller coasters of emotions when things are lost and then found.

 Luke 15:1-7

This passage is rich with treasures straight from Jesus. The parable of Jesus going after the one lost sheep should fill us with inordinate joy. He wants you to belong to Him, so much that He left the flock to come for you! I thought about calling this book *Leaving the Ninety-Nine for You*. The fact that Jesus cares so much for the lost is a priceless and inexplicable gift.

Let me give you some background about the importance of a

shepherd. I read a book by Phillip Keller, who spent his early life as a shepherd. The book gave me so much insight! The shepherd was everything to the sheep. He protected them, and he found pastureland for them. The shepherd positioned himself as their guard in the sheep pen. He put oil on their heads to protect them from flies, and he could take out a predator with one sling of a rock.

With that background, read this again: *³ Then Jesus told them this parable: ⁴ "Suppose one of you has a hundred sheep and loses one of them. Doesn't he leave the ninety-nine in the open country and go after the lost sheep until he finds it? ⁵ And when he finds it, he joyfully puts it on his shoulders ⁶ and goes home. Then he calls his friends and neighbors together and says, 'Rejoice with me; I have found my lost sheep.' ⁷ I tell you that in the same way there will be more rejoicing in heaven over one sinner who repents than over ninety-nine righteous persons who do not need to repent."* My friends, that is how much our Savior loves you! Can you believe that Jesus said that there is more rejoicing over one **lost** person repenting than over the ninety-nine righteous people praising God? Jesus certainly wasn't one to mince words. If this doesn't cause you to do a bit of self-assessment, perhaps it should. I know it does for me. Jesus wanted to ensure this message sank in, so He explained it another way.

 Luke 15:8-10

In this teaching the woman lost one of her ten coins. However, she didn't simply forget about the coin because the coin was valuable to her. One silver coin at that time was worth one day's wages. Once she found it, she called her friends and neighbors and exclaimed, *⁹ "Rejoice with me!"* We would not call friends to rejoice over something of little value. However, we would call them to rejoice if it were something that meant a lot to us. This parable is meant to show us how much God cares for us; we are of immense value to Him. Once again, we see the theme of the value of the lost being found. Re-read verse 10: *"In the same way, I tell you, there is rejoicing in the presence of the angels of God over one sinner who repents."* This clearly emphasizes the truth of how much **value God puts in the lost being found!**

 Luke 15:11-31

Let's look at this passage from three different perspectives. First, from the father in the story. Some of you reading this may understand the father because you are a parent or grandparent. Put yourself in the shoes of this father for a minute. Imagine your son came to you and said, "Dad, Mom, I know you're not dead, but I really don't want to stay around home anymore. I want you to give me my share of your wealth so I can hit the road." Not many of us, if any, would do this. Keep in mind that this is a parable, a story, given to us by Jesus to teach us about God, not based on the realistic likelihood of this happening today.

This shows us that God is far more generous with us than we would likely ever be. He is willing to do things that most of us would never do. God is fully aware of the fact that we will make bad choices, sin, and make mistakes. He knows the fray we are going to wind up in. Yet He still allows us to find our way through it. Imagine the pain of having a child who, through their actions, expresses to you that they don't care about you. They express that they only care about what they can get from you. That would hurt terribly, and maybe some of you understand the pain from first-hand experience. This is the pain we put God through every time we willingly sin. This is like telling God that you know what you are doing is wrong, but your desire in this moment is greater than the concept of a distant heaven and eternal life. The here and now takes precedence over a future of everlasting misery.

Put on the dad's shoes one more time. Imagine you are generous and give your son the money. The son then takes off only to slide into a lifestyle of horrible choices. As the parent, wouldn't you ask questions like, "How could the child I loved be acting like this? Or how could the child I raised live a life they know is wrong? How could my precious child do drugs or use their body this way?" Then imagine they fall off the grid completely, and you lose track of them. Our question then becomes, "Are they dead? Who are they living with? Where are they?" Some of you have experienced this, but hopefully the rest of you will never know this pain. Like most parents, this father waited up, praying that everything was okay and that his son would come home.

Now look at how this father, who represents God, responded when his son finally came home. Compare it to how you act when your son or daughter sneaks in after curfew. [20] *"But while he was still a long way off, his father saw him and was filled with compassion for him; he ran to his son, threw his arms around him and kissed him."* Is that how most parents would respond? Probably not. God responds differently. God doesn't hold our sin against us like we, all too often, do against our children.

The father does not respond to his son's apology. He doesn't question what he has been doing or lecture him on how terrible he was for doing what he did. The father does not scream at him or hit him. The father hugs him, kisses him, and calls for a party to be thrown in honor of his lost son who has returned. This might differ from how your parents treated you, but what an incredible model it is of a loving father!

The second perspective I want us to consider is that of the son. Put yourself in the shoes of the prodigal son. Imagine growing up in a house with a dad whom you thought was super religious, the type of dad who always wanted you to walk the straight and narrow path. Meanwhile, you wanted to go and have some fun and live life on your terms. The Bible said this of his son: [13] *"Squandered his wealth in wild living."* He lived up to the name the Bible gave him, A.K.A., the Prodigal Son, which means to live rashly and wastefully. We know this kind of life almost always ends badly. His dream life became his worst nightmare. [15] *"So he went and hired himself out to a citizen of that country, who sent him to his fields to feed pigs. [16] He longed to fill his stomach with the pods that the pigs were eating, but no one gave him anything."*

What can we learn from this passage? The son reached a point in his life where he actually hit rock bottom. He thought back to his father's servants and how well they were fed and taken care of by his father. He knew that he could not go back as a son because of what he had done... but perhaps he could go back as a servant. [20] *"So he got up and went to his father. But while he was still a long way off, his father saw him and was filled with compassion for him; he ran to his son, threw his arms around him and kissed him. [21] "The son said to him, 'Father, I have sinned against heaven and against you. I am no longer worthy to be called your son."* The father didn't answer; the father didn't accuse. He threw a party instead. The lost had been found!

You may be running from your parents, from the past, from a job or a relationship because you don't want to be hurt again. You may be addicted to gambling, alcohol, drugs, food, gossip, or backstabbing people at work. You may be in a terrible co-dependent relationship. Any of these things or dozens of others lead to this question: **What is keeping you from being who God created you to be?**

There is one more perspective to consider in this story: the good son. Maybe you are the good son or daughter in your family. I definitely was not. Maybe you are the one who didn't wander away from your parents' training. If that is you, there is a message in this story for you as well. The prodigal son had a good brother.

While the prodigal son was partying his life away, the good son was doing what good sons do: working hard and following the rules. When the good son returned, he heard the sounds of a party. Now, put yourself in the good son's shoes. Your selfish, wasteful little brother finally came home because he was probably looking for another handout. And you know he has never done one good thing in his entire life. While you always follow the straight and narrow path, he does the polar opposite.

Understand, the good son's facts are not wrong. That being said, his feelings and heart are far from being godly, which is why his father responds with this: *[31] "'My son,' the father said, 'you are always with me, and everything I have is yours. [32] But we had to celebrate and be glad, because this brother of yours was dead and is alive again; he was lost and is found.'"* And there is that phrase about lost people again. Why does God keep going there? Why is it always about the lost being found? Could it be because every person is lost at one point? Maybe you are still lost and searching for a way to come home. God loves you so much that He will do anything to help you come to understand that Jesus is the real, living Son of God. He wants to be your Savior and to forgive you for all the wrongs you have done.

The problem we have in the modern American church is that we have far too many people who could care less about reaching lost people with the Good News of Jesus Christ. They have made a hobby out of acting like the good son. They love to complain to God and others about how those lost people don't act like us Christians. How those lost people don't like our music. How those lost people's kids don't behave correctly. How those lost people don't take care of things like they should. The good sons perceive that the lost are worthless to God and the Kingdom because of the choices they have made in life. At the same time, God is saying, "Can't you see that eternity is yours? Everything I have is yours! I love the lost, too, and I need you to love them as well."

Let me make this perfectly clear for those who see themselves as the good son-type Christians…Who cares if new people don't like your style of music, or if they are rougher on the church building, or if they don't dress like you. God is begging His children to see how awesome it is when the lost come to know Jesus and are found! Look through God's eyes; that is His goal for you. Let's end with one last question: **Is your heart aligned with God's heart for the lost?**

LIFE APPLICATION

- Examine your heart this week. Who/where are you in this story, and what do you need to do either in your life or in the life of someone you know to grow closer to Jesus?
- In today's reading, what did you learn about God, yourself, and mankind?
- As a result of today's reading, how will you apply what you learned? Answer as I will…

CHAPTER 56

WHAT'S LOVE GOT TO DO WITH IT?

 John 11:1-6

Throughout the course of your life, have you ever said something you did not mean to say? In the heat of the moment, most of us blurt things out. While commonly used, "in the heat of the moment" is a cop-out. It may be when you say something unintended but you really do mean it. What you believe about God, what you really believe about yourself—it bubbles up in those moments and slips through your lips. When life gets difficult, challenging, or intense, and when situations escalate, what you really believe, what you thought you would never say, but maybe what you think about a lot—that comes out!

 John 11:1-5

Mary and Martha were in the middle of one of those really hard times. Their beloved little brother, Lazarus, was on death's doorstep. They had explored all other avenues to save him but decided there was only one thing that could help—a miracle. They knew Jesus was a miracle worker and that He could save their brother. They needed Jesus to come and heal Lazarus. Mary and Martha wrote a short note, put it in a messenger's hand, and waited for the messenger to find Jesus. They **believed** Jesus would read it, come right away, and save their little brother's life.

This tells us what Mary and Martha believed about Jesus. When push came to shove, when it was a matter of life and death, what Mary and Martha believed was about to become reality. Bear in mind that Mary, Martha, and Lazarus were like family to

Jesus, so much so that the second-to-last week of Jesus's life was spent with them. They were that close with Jesus. That is why they knew Jesus would come to save Lazarus.

As I was reading this passage, I got to verse three and read, *³ Lord, the one you love is sick.* Something hit me… why was the note so short? I thought about myself, and what if this were my brother? If it were my brother, I would put more details in my letter, more pleading on why it was so important that Jesus come now! When my dad and my son got cancer, I can tell you my prayers were longer than "Hey, God, the ones you love, AKA my dad and son, are sick."

If I had only one note to write to save my loved one's life, I would instantly share why this message was so critical. I would remind Jesus that my brother had kids, and, of course, He wouldn't let them grow up without a father. I would plead with God and give reasons why He should save my brother's life. That is what most of us would do if we were in Mary and Martha's shoes.

Read again what they said: *³ Lord, the one you love is sick.* The end. Nothing more needed. This was what Mary and Martha believed was sufficient information. They believed what would move Jesus the most was His love for Lazarus, not Lazarus' love for Him. Let that sink in. **Mary and Martha believed what would move Jesus the most was His love for Lazarus, not Lazarus' love for Him.** That is why they said, "the one YOU (referring to Jesus) love." When that reality hit me, my eyes got misty. Why do we always slip into life being all about us? Why do we forget life is about God? Life is about God's love and God's love for us. Here is the point: **Love moves God.**

So as this was swirling around in my mind, I found myself asking this question: **"What is the focus of the gospel?"** The gospel means the Good News of what God has done through Jesus. What was the main focus or the point of Jesus' life? We are getting down to the final stretch of it. If you had to boil it down to one thing, what would it be? Or we can look at it from another perspective. You may know the meaning of the word gospel, but have you ever looked at your life and considered what your life says by the way you are living? Have you asked yourself what your greatest priorities are and do they accurately portray what you believe? **The essence of the Gospel is overwhelmingly God's love for mankind.**

Here is a thought that could change your entire outlook on God and life: What would you say moves God the most? It could be anything, nothing, judgment, joy, fear, courage, prayers, or His own agenda. Consider the idea that God is moved to the greatest extent by His own love. God's ways are higher than our ways. His love is higher than our love. God loves bad and broken people. God is obsessed with reaching sinners. Let me ask you something that is hard, based on our modern world. **What is love without freedom? What is love without choice?**

We all know the answer to that. We have a word for it. Without choice, without free will to choose love, without freedom, we have lost the definition of love. In our culture, forced love takes you to one place: jail. Forced love isn't love at all; it is abuse and manipulation. Real love is never forced upon you. **God is not abusive, God does not manipulate, and God gives you free will to accept His love.**

You can either acknowledge this love extended to you or ignore it. The choice is yours, but His love will always remain. God is love. The entire Bible is God's love story for His creation. The Bible is all about God, not man. Once we realize that life is not about us, we can see that we have had things out of order. We notice that our constant focus on our performance, our deeds, or our efforts was never the point of life.

Mary and Martha made it abundantly clear when they used the word love in their note: *³ Lord, the one you love is sick.*

The love Mary and Martha expressed is referred to as *phileo*.

Phileo is an earthly best friend-type of love. *Phileo* is love that is based upon reciprocation. You give love, and you get love in return. Mary and Martha wrote the note to Jesus and essentially said, "The one that you love, and who loves you back, is sick." Mary and Martha were wrong because God does not love anyone with a *phileo* type of love. He never has, and He never will! God has a love that is exclusively His. It flows from His being. It is the essence of who He is, and it is not dependent on reciprocation. It is otherworldly love, from another realm, from another dimension, from the essence and core of His being. God does not feel love. God does not merely express love. God is love! God is *agape*, a love that absolutely does not need any reciprocation. It is unconditional, it is relentless, and it is persistent.

This is God. He has *agape* love for every human being that has ever lived. God does not *phileo* humanity; God *agapes* humanity. Amazingly, God is so relentless in *agape* love for us that He will not stop loving us. God cannot help Himself. How ridiculous is this love! How extensive and how extraordinary is this God's love!

We've got to get the message out that if even you are right in the middle of sin, God is still relentless in His *agape* love for you. He can't help Himself. He created you. His love remains no matter what you do. I pray for you to be preoccupied with God's extraordinary, extensive, and expansive love for you. God's love never fails. It never quits. For as long as God exists (which is forever), His love for you remains. What an extraordinary love.

Let's read one last verse, John 11:6. *So when he heard that Lazarus was sick, he stayed where he was two more days.* What? Jesus heard that one of his best friends was sick, and He didn't head straight his way? Why? That's because His plans are always greater than ours, and the best is yet to come!

 **LIFE APPLICATION**

- How could you model agape love to others in such a way that it could cause them to notice a difference in how you love people, thus helping point them toward God?
- In today's reading, what did you learn about God, yourself, and mankind?
- As a result of today's reading, how will you apply what you learned? Answer as I will…

CHAPTER 57

THE BEST IS YET TO COME

 John 11:1-40, Matthew 4:23

There was a young woman who had been diagnosed with a terminal illness and had been given three months to live. She contacted her pastor and had him come to her house to discuss certain aspects of her final wishes. She told him which songs and Scriptures she wanted and what outfit she wanted to be buried in. When the pastor was preparing to leave, the young woman suddenly remembered something very important to her. "There's one more thing," she said excitedly. "What's that?" came the Pastor's reply. She said, "I want a fork in my right hand in the casket." The Pastor looked at the young woman, not knowing what to say.

"That surprises you, doesn't it?" the young woman said. "Well, to be honest, I'm puzzled by the request," the Pastor answered. The young woman explained, "My grandmother once told me this story, and from that time on I have always tried to pass along its message to those I love and those who need encouragement. My grandmother always told me about her years of attending socials and dinners. She said that when the main course dishes were being cleared, someone would inevitably lean over and say, 'Keep your fork because the best is yet to come.' I want people to see me there in that casket with a fork in my hand and I want them to wonder, 'What's with the fork?' Then I want you to tell them at the end of my service, 'Keep your fork because the best is yet to come.' This is a great reminder that heaven is right around the corner, and we should never forget the best part of our lives is coming when we go to meet Jesus!" When we are walking with Jesus, the best is always yet to come!

Matthew 4:23 applies to what we will be talking about, so let's start there. *Jesus went throughout Galilee, teaching in their synagogues, proclaiming the good news of the kingdom, and healing every disease and sickness among the people.* Other translations say "healing every affliction." God has a message for you amid whatever is afflicting you or causing you pain. I want you to understand something right out of the gate: **God does not inflict anything on us.** God knows everything you and I will ever do. Even with that foreknowledge of the messes and sins we may find ourselves in, God does not inflict anything on us.

God is so loving that even though He knows what you will do in your future and knows what you did at every point in your past, He will not inflict judgment in your present. That is extraordinary to me. This concept is so different from how our world works. If someone did something to hurt us in our past, we assume they will do it again. Sadly, many people assume the worst of people far more often than they assume the best. But God has this extraordinary and inexplicable love that waits for our return, forgives us expansively, and unconditionally looks out for our best interests. God always believes that our best is yet to come, just like the story of the fork.

Read Matthew 4:23 again. *Jesus went throughout Galilee, teaching in their synagogues, proclaiming the good news of the kingdom, and healing every disease and sickness among the people.* Note the word "every." Note also what it did not say. It did not say deserving, or godly, or good sick people. It didn't say righteous or religious sick people. It didn't say only Jesus' followers and devout Christians. It said that He healed every sick person, every disease, and every affliction among the people. Some of them may have done evil or terrible things. God may have healed hands that would be used to hurt someone in the future. He may have healed eyes that would lust. He may have healed feet that would run away from Him and His commandments. This makes many of us wonder why Jesus would spend His time and energy on broken and lost people.

What would you do if you were God? Would you heal someone if you had the foreknowledge that they would hurt someone you loved? I would boot them from the line, and likely you would, too. That is one of many reasons why I am grateful that you and I are not God. His ways and His perspectives are greater and more loving that ours could ever be. The reality is that we have all hurt someone God loves. All of this leads us back to our passage from the last chapter because we need to finish the story about this friend of Jesus who was about to die.

 John 11:1-5

Jesus received the note to come help one of His friends who was at death's door, but He didn't go to him immediately. He stayed where He was for two more days. Jesus was apparently in no hurry to get to His friend's house, and because he waited, His friend Lazarus died. If you are like me, you might ask, "Why did Jesus wait?"

Many believe Jesus waited because Jewish people believed that by the fourth day after death, there was no hope for a person to return to life. That was their custom. When the fourth day came, there was officially no hope, and they would bury the body. The Jews believed there was absolutely no coming back after the fourth day. They believed their spirit was gone. Jesus waited two days because the trip to Lazarus' house would take Him another two days. That meant His friend was officially dead. Jesus was not waiting around for the sake of waiting. He wasn't like that one family member we all know who is always late. He waited for a specific purpose. **Jesus was waiting to show his friends and the world that He had power over life and death.**

Let me give you a picture of the kind of dedication and purpose that will help you remember this. Growing up, my brothers and I discovered that my mom was amazingly easy to scare. We used to have so much fun doing things like hiding a life-sized cardboard cutout of Star Wars characters behind corners and doors to surprise her. We found great joy in hearing our mom scream like someone was attacking her. My wife Jenny, who is amazing, is also easy to scare. I have trouble staying still (having Attention Deficit Disorder doesn't help with that), but there have been times when I have hidden in the perfect spot for so long that I got cramps waiting with purpose to spring out and scare my wonderful wife. Hopefully, that helps you never forget this passage. I learned this art of waiting for a purpose from Jesus.

 John 11:7-37

Jesus arrived on day four. Lazarus had no chance of coming back to life. In verses 18-22, you can hear Martha's faith; she knew Jesus **could have** healed her brother but that too much time had passed. She still did not understand that Jesus was God, but she had faith that He could do something miraculous. Mary said the same thing. *³² When Mary reached the place where Jesus was and saw him, she fell at his feet and said, "Lord, if you had been here, my brother would not have died."*

Let me draw your attention to something else that was very odd. Jesus came down the road, seemingly too late but with a purpose. He talked with Martha and Mary and asked where Lazarus was laid. Then we read the shortest verse in the New Testament: *³⁵ Jesus wept.* Jesus went there to heal Lazarus. He knew why He was there. He knew what He was about to do, yet He took time to pause and cry. Why?

Everyone who was there looked at Jesus crying. *³⁶ Then the Jews said, "See how he loved him!" ³⁷ But some of them said, "Could not he who opened the eyes of the blind man have kept this man from dying?"* The first time I read this, I remember thinking, "Why is Jesus getting all emotional?" Is it just me, or does that seem odd to you? Why did He weep? When I am confused by a Bible verse, I ask God to give me clarity. Then I begin digging into other Bible passages to see if they provide any answers. As I have said before, I do not like crying. Perhaps that was why I needed to figure this out. I even asked God if I should be a crier. Then it dawned on me! He cried because **God's love is always in the here and now.**

Was Mary and Martha's pain lessened in that moment when they were speaking with Jesus? Their pain was real and raw. What does this show us about God? Jesus does not walk up and say, "Oh, Mary, Martha, stop it. I am here now. Come on, Lazarus is going to be fine." Jesus doesn't tell them to act a certain way or expect them to immediately stop grieving upon His arrival.

This passage shows us that God has such extraordinary love for humanity that He takes time to cry with us. God shares our grief! He understands what we are going through, and He never leaves us in our pain. He understands that even when we lose someone who is now in the perfection of eternity, we still mourn. In moments like this, remember that the resurrection of Jesus changed everything.

One day we will be in eternity with those who have passed before us. We all hope to see them in heaven one day. Heaven should be a central theme of our existence on this planet. When our loved ones are gone, like Lazarus was gone, we are only separated temporarily. Yes, the pain is real, deep, challenging, and even overwhelming. Yet in those times of despair, Jesus says to you, just like he did to Mary and Martha, "Come here and let's cry together." God knows everything, and He will weep with you because His love is always present and available. In this story, Jesus showed His compassion and His extraordinary love for us as God.

John 11:38-44

Imagine being Mary or Martha at that moment the impossible happened before their eyes! Their brother was lost to them, and now he has returned! Crazy emotions must have been running through their minds and bodies. Imagine being one of the people, there mourning with them, who saw this happen. We would be amazed! Perhaps it is an overreach to say the best is yet to come here on earth, but the closer we get to our Savior Jesus, it certainly feels that way.

Let me wrap this up with an illustration about parenting. Parenting is a unique experience. I have four children. I love my kids. They are gloriously awesome, wonderful, and, frankly, challenging. Recently, I was missing the days when they were younger. I missed how Addie would say "snugs" instead of slugs. I missed Thatcher's long, crazy mop of hair. I missed how Wyatt always wore his shirts, shorts, and pants backwards. I missed how Belle always wanted to be with us and never cared about having friends. I missed... I missed... I missed...

Parenting is incredible; yet, we find ourselves thinking things like, "I can't wait until we're out of diapers, or out of a car seat, when they can ride a bike with me, or feed themselves, or drive themselves," and the cycle goes on and on. I remember the Holy Spirit nudging me that day and asking me, "Adam, what do you want? Do you want to go back, do you want to go forward, or do you want to enjoy the here and now?"

God is a "right here" God. God is a "right now" God. Jesus taught us that. He told us not to worry about tomorrow. Enjoy today. Enjoy God's present love. God is with you, God is for you, and God loves you. However, God is also a future God. He has a plan and purpose for our future. I don't know what you're going through. I don't pretend for a moment to understand what you're facing, or the challenges and trials in your life. Even still, I sense that the Holy Spirit is trying to nudge you to relax a little bit and let go of your worries. Lean into His love and let yourself live today. We will be in heaven before we know it, this life will be over, and the best will have come. God was in your past, He will sit with you today in your praise or your lament, and He has a hope for your tomorrow. He knows what you're going through, so lean into Him. Communicate with Him. Talk with Him. God loves you so much. Keep your fork because every day with Him will be better than the day before! By walking with and trusting God, the best is always on the horizon.

 LIFE APPLICATION

- How could your life look different if you approached it with the mentality that with God, the best is yet to come? How can you rejoice in what is going on in your life today?
- In today's reading, what did you learn about God, yourself, and mankind?
- As a result of today's reading, how will you apply what you learned? Answer as I will…

CHAPTER 58

A WARNING, FORGIVENESS, & THANKFULNESS

 Luke 17

When I was in high school, I had a friend who did not know Jesus. I invited him to our youth group, and he accepted the invitation. We were goofing off while the janitor was still there working, and he really berated my friend about goofing off in God's house. Our youth pastor calmed him down and tried to smooth things over, but that was the end of my friend's interest in the youth group. To this day, I tell everyone that we want kids to be comfortable in church buildings, so if they get a little rambunctious, please be gentle and kind. In this passage, Jesus warns us about doing things that can cause kids to move away from God.

 Luke 17:1-10

Jesus gave a powerful warning to never cause the little ones to stumble. This meant that we must not stand in the way of children, or the spiritually young, in coming to know Jesus. In today's culture this can happen in endless ways. The younger generation has less and less interest in church, often for reasons that have nothing to do with Jesus. Surveys tell us it is the rigidity of the church that is responsible for their lack of interest. This strict culture might include rules such as no hats in church, irrelevant and outdated music, criticism of their dyed hair, or body shaming of their tattoos. Jesus was different than that. **Jesus cares more about lost people and children coming to know Him than what they wear, look like, or how they act in religious settings.**

Jesus also said, *³ "If your brother or sister sins against you, rebuke them; and if they repent, forgive them. ⁴ Even if they sin against you seven times in a day and seven times come back to you saying 'I repent,' you must forgive them."* Have you ever wanted to ask Jesus how many times you must forgive someone? You may have questions for Jesus such as, "What is the limit? When do I get to say enough is enough and write the person off? What if they keep making the same mistakes?" The answer is simple. Jesus clearly said that **we must never withhold forgiveness.**

I love the next part of this story and even though we have touched on this before, there is still more to glean from it. *¹¹ Now on his way to Jerusalem, Jesus traveled along the border between Samaria and Galilee. ¹² As he was going into a village, ten men who had leprosy met him. They stood at a distance ¹³ and called out in a loud voice, "Jesus, Master, have pity on us!" ¹⁴ When he saw them, he said, "Go, show yourselves to the priests."* This story began with ten men who had the worst disease of their day, with no hope of a cure. Put yourself in their shoes. Imagine that you have a disease where you are slowly losing feeling in your body. You literally begin to lose parts of your body. You are forced to be separated from all people, including your family. This is because leprosy was so contagious that there could be no contact whatsoever with anyone, including their children, grandchildren, or spouse. Think about the horrible emotional, physical, and psychological pain they endured.

Since they could not come close, they screamed to Jesus, *¹³ "Have pity on us!"* The Great Teacher said, *¹⁴ "Go and show yourselves to the priest."* They looked down at their bodies. The hands of one man were still mangled. Another man looked at his leg, which ended with a filthy rag at the knee. Another looked at his skin and found it as repulsive as ever. In other words, all these men were no better off than they had been a minute earlier when they first spotted Jesus.

Would you have listened to Jesus even when it did not make

sense? Would you do what He said even if nothing in your life had changed and nothing was better at that moment? Pay attention to the main point here. For this miracle to happen, these men had to start walking in faith before their circumstances would change.

You cannot wait until your problems are over to start walking in faith. You cannot put conditions on God. You cannot say, "Lord, as soon as there's enough money, I'll follow your instructions and tithe." You cannot pray, "Lord, if you'll just solve this issue in my family, then I'll start going to church." You cannot barter with God.

Instead, God places a faith expectation on us, sometimes before He changes anything in our lives. God might say, "Love me despite the disease. Try out for the team even though you think you lack talent. Start the business even though you lack resources. Follow me now, despite what is missing. Say "no" to the temptation while it is still difficult. Praise me in the darkest of nights and in the worst of circumstances. Be thankful when nothing about your circumstances gives you that motivation." That is the very definition of faith. If you praise God only on the good days in only the best of circumstances, you are not putting your faith into practice. Be thankful despite the difficult circumstances and trust in God's perfect timing.

Jesus told these men to *[14] "Go and show yourselves to the priest. And as they went, they were cleansed."* Do you see what happened? Jesus healed them AFTER they stepped out in faith! They had to start walking BEFORE the healing came! Their walking out in faith was essential for seeing changes in their lives.

These ten men with leprosy pleaded with Jesus to pity them. Jesus healed all ten of them, but did you notice what happened afterward? *[15] One of them, when he saw he was healed, came back, praising God in a loud voice. [16] He threw himself at Jesus' feet and thanked him—and he was a Samaritan. [17] Jesus asked, "Were not all ten cleansed? Where are the other nine? [18] Has no one returned to give praise to God except this foreigner?" ⁹¹ Then he said to him, "Rise and go; your faith has made you well."* Jesus knew how many would return and thank him, but He still healed all ten. Jesus made a point of this to remind us that thankfulness to God is expected. Often, gratitude is lacking in the heart of mankind. If we truly love Jesus, we must **make sure our thankfulness leads to action.**

One healed leper's gratitude led to action. That leper caught himself in the midst of the celebration. He reversed his steps, put his family on hold, put the priest on hold, and returned to the cause of his healing. Jesus never commanded that any of them express thankfulness to God or return to Him, the source of their healing. Nevertheless, that is what Jesus expected.

What kind of action is Jesus looking for from you? Has the Holy Spirit been urging you toward some action step? Has the Lord been tugging at you for some step of faith? Is there a family, a friend, or even a stranger needing help? Is there something you feel compelled to do? **Living a thankful life, a faith-filled life, and an action-filled life leads to a life of spiritual wellness.**

Then Jesus said to this very thankful man, *¹⁹ "Rise and go; your faith has made you well."* Jesus pronounced a complete healing that came from a spiritual source: the leper's faith. This was wellness of the soul, the one thing that no medicine or person can heal but God alone. No matter what you are going through today, you can be made well in a way that cannot be described. Our healing begins by acknowledging Jesus for who He is and what He alone can do.

 LIFE APPLICATION

- Is there something you should be thanking God for? Is there something you know God wants you to do that you have

avoided? Make time to thank God and follow His lead.
- In today's reading, what did you learn about God, yourself, and mankind?
- As a result of today's reading, how will you apply what you learned? Answer as I will…

CHAPTER 59

PRAYER, RIGHTEOUSNESS, & RICHES

 Luke 18

As a pastor, I have been with many people as they are nearing the end of life. Listening to their conversations is fascinating; the small talk about football or sewing is gone. Those who are near death get down to the deep issues that really matter, the issues they want their loved ones to remember when they are gone. If they lived a godly life, I often hear them speak important God-ordained words to those they love. Even those who do not believe in God tend to want to pass along a nugget of wisdom to their children and grandchildren. As we approach the end of Jesus' life, we will also see Him tackling some tough topics, so lean in and learn as much as you can.

In this chapter's Bible passage, Jesus will begin by discussing the Kingdom of God. Then He talks about investing in the Kingdom of God. He will wrap it up with some intense words. Jesus was, at times, very intense and not always matching the persona our current culture promotes. Jesus was about love. However, He never said anyone is free to do whatever they like as long as it makes them happy. He never preached a purely sunshine and rainbow sermon. Jesus understood that there is a real place called heaven and a real place called hell. His mission was to come to earth and make disciples who would build God's Kingdom, not their own. This message is not an easy one but it is a critical one. You are about to read two parables. Remember that a parable is an illustration with a moral or spiritual lesson.

Luke 18:1-8

Luke 18:1-8 is a part of Jesus' teaching on the end times. Jesus closed with the question: *⁸ "When the Son of man comes, will he find faith on earth?"* His disciples likely asked a few questions about the end times. There are a few questions we should probably ask, too. How can we endure to the end? How can we ensure we don't become like Lot's wife (Genesis 19)? How do we ensure we don't love this world more than Jesus? How can we resist the relentless temptations of Sodom, or America? How can we keep from becoming desensitized to God's Kingdom? How can we overcome the ordinary pressures of daily life?

The danger we face is that our faith in Jesus, our love for Jesus, can be swallowed up by daily life. How can we endure and be found full of faith and love at the end of our lives? This is one of the few parables where Jesus gave us the answer. Jesus told His disciples a parable to show them that *¹ they should always pray and not give up.* There *is* the answer, and here *is* the point: **If we want to remain in Jesus to the end, the key is to pray and pray and pray, and not ever grow weary of praying.**

This parable was intended to encourage us to pray continually until Jesus comes back. When Jesus asked at the end of verse 8, *"However, when the Son of Man comes, will he find faith on the earth?"* Jesus asked, "Will I come back and find my disciples praying, or will they have lost heart and given up?" He was clearly implying that prayer and faith stand or fall together.

Faith is the furnace of our lives and the coal feeding that furnace inside us is prayer. If you lose heart and lay down the shovel designed for putting coal in the fire, that fire will go out. We will grow cold and hard if we lose heart and stop praying. Remember the following warning from Jesus: When Jesus returns and appears in all His glory, He said He will spew lukewarm people out of His mouth (Revelation 3:16). Matthew 24:13 says, *but the one who stand firms to the end will be saved.* That is why Jesus said **prayer is essential to life.**

 Luke 18:9-14

This was directed at people who were confident of their goodness. They believed they were godly people. Perhaps they were also people who looked down on others whom they assumed were less godly. This attitude can be seen in many people today. It is hard to love people who do not act, look, live, or have the same political views as us. It is hard to live out a life of simply loving people so radically that they become disciples of Jesus Christ. It was hard in Jesus' time and it is still hard today.

Now let's direct our attention to a critical point. *⁹ To some who were confident of their own righteousness and looked down on everyone else, Jesus told this parable:* Note the first words. It does not say that Jesus told this parable **about** people who trusted in themselves and were righteous. Jesus said this **to** people who trusted in themselves and in their own righteousness. Jesus was looking these people in the eye and telling them that they were self-righteous. He was not talking about them behind their backs, like so many do. It is easy to talk about people when they are not around. Some even find it fun to gossip about people behind their backs because they can't correct or criticize you when you talk about them. They are not there to defend themselves. Jesus shows us the right way—**Jesus spoke directly to them!**

Next, Jesus gave an illustration that would have been shocking to hear. *¹¹ "The Pharisee stood by himself and prayed: 'God, I thank you that I am not like other people—robbers, evildoers, adulterers—or even like this tax collector.'"* Do you hear yourself saying, "Thank you, God, that I am not like those kinds of people." *¹² "'I fast twice a week and give a tenth of all I get.'"* Do you hear yourself saying,

"I do the things I define as important and that makes me a good person." From a Jewish perspective, this Pharisee did all the right stuff, and the tax collector did all the wrong stuff. *¹³ "But the tax collector stood at a distance. He would not even look up to heaven, but beat his breast and said, 'God, have mercy on me, a sinner.'"* The tax collector demonstrated a heart seeking to change and align with God's design for life.

Put yourself in this scene. Jesus was looking right into the eyes of extremely religious people who talked endlessly about God and who thought they were doing the proper religious rituals and activities. However, they didn't realize that everything written about God in the Old Testament was pointing to a Redeemer, a Savior, a sacrifice—everything pointed to Jesus.

Jesus came to reveal Himself, but they could not see Him. They knew about God. They knew about grace. They knew about righteousness. But they missed the one true God made into flesh. They did not understand justification by faith alone.*¹⁴ "I tell you that this man, rather than the other, went home justified before God. For all those who exalt themselves will be humbled, and those who humble themselves will be exalted."*

Who do you look down on? Who do you think you are better than? Do you believe that your religious activities, lifestyle, political beliefs, career, or financial position make you better than others? If we are being honest with ourselves, we would probably say that we have felt this way at some point in our lives. This man was like many of us reading this. He was a good church-going person. He was doing the right things according to his culture. What we missed is that Jesus was making a point about motives—this man had the wrong motive.

In verse 14, we find that this man trusted the wrong thing. He was looking at the wrong thing for his righteousness. The biggest mistake he made was looking at the wrong person. He thought it was about his personal righteous behavior. He was not presented as a legalist. That was not the issue. This man was morally upright and religiously devout. He believed God made him, and since God entrusted him with wealth, he honored God and gave back to God. He gave thanks to God. He was praying to God in the place where he worshiped God at the moment of this story. Even with his well-intended practices, he was dead wrong in his beliefs, and so are many people today.

Those who are turning from justification by faith in Jesus' sacrifice alone are wrong. Jesus wanted us to learn that it is not about how righteous, moral, and religious we are. It is not about whether you give God the first 10% of your money or not. The key is not whether you are a better person than others around you. That is not the basis of your justification before God. That is not how you are accepted and declared righteous in God's court of law. We must look at and trust in Jesus and all that God did through Him alone.

The tax collector in this parable symbolizes the worst of sinners in Jesus' culture. That would be like a mass murderer or whoever you consider to be the worst of sinners today. The tax collector looked away from himself and toward God for redemption. The sinner did not trust in anything he did. He knew he was broken. The sinner trusted in God. Do not miss what Jesus said: *14 "I tell you that this man, rather than the other, went home justified before God."* Here is the main point: **Truly righteous people understand they are broken and saved by Christ alone.**

 Luke 18:18-30

It is interesting that we just read about another moral person asking the same question with the same answer. We need to learn that apart from God, we do nothing of worth. *28 Peter said to him, "We have left all we had to follow you!" 29 "Truly I tell you,"* Jesus *said to them, "no one who has left home or wife or brothers or sisters or parents or children for the sake of the kingdom of God [30] will fail to receive many times as much in this age, and in the age to come eternal life."*

This could have been my story before I was in ministry. Even by American standards, we were becoming rich at a young age. I was a good person. I went to church and was in seminary. Overall, I was a good moral person, doing good things and making lots of money, just like this guy. Similar to the man in the passage, Jesus asked me, my wife, and my family to leave it all and follow Him. I had to decide to walk away from a fantastic career. This was probably the hardest decision my wife and I have ever made.

It is so hard to say to Jesus, "Okay, yes, I will step out in faith and completely trust You." My wife and I felt God speak to us, "If you really believe this life is just the foundation of eternity, what will you give up for Me?" After talking about that, we said, "God, we will give you everything we have." We felt God say, "Then give Me everything you have."

We decided to do it, to invest in the kingdom to come, to play the long game, which everyone reading this does as well, just not always in reference to eternal life. That is why you have a retirement account, savings account, etc. You defer today's desires for the theory of a better future. **Where are you going to invest?** If this life is the foundation of what is to come, what wouldn't you give up for God? My wife and I gave up a lot for God from a worldly perspective, but I can assure you that we both feel like God has been immeasurably good to us since then, and I cannot wait to see our reward in heaven!

By the grace of God, He helped us leave that life behind and not choose as this rich young man did. It was the best decision we ever made and we have never regretted it. God wants every person to follow His direction for their life. That does NOT mean God will call everyone to leave everything for Him. It means God does not want to be second place to anything else in your life. For me, my money and my career came before God. Those things mattered more to me than God did. So, God had to take them away from me. Looking back, I am so glad He did.

 LIFE APPLICATION

- What is of the greatest importance in your life? If you give up something in your life that you think you cannot give up, it will bring you freedom. It brought me freedom. I want you to be free, too!
- In today's reading, what did you learn about God, yourself, and mankind?
- As a result of today's reading, how will you apply what you learned? Answer as I will…

_____
_____
_____
_____
_____
_____
_____
_____
_____
_____
_____

CHAPTER 60

JESUS TEACHES ON DIVORCE

 Matthew 19:1-12, Mark 10:1-12

Divorce is an epidemic that statistics tell us affects about half of all people reading this book. Jesus spoke the following words to His disciples two thousand years ago, and they still apply to our lives today, even if our culture says they do not. As a side note, when Jesus said this 2000 years ago, it would not have been in harmony with His culture either.

 Matthew 19:1-12

The Bible teaches us quite a bit about marriage. If we believe in the Word of God, we will find that God's design for marriage has always been a lifelong commitment to one spouse of the opposite sex. We must keep a clear, biblical, and eternal perspective and remind ourselves repeatedly that, compared to eternal life with God, this earthly life, whether single or married, divorced or not, is truly short compared to eternity. I know it does not feel that way at this moment, which is why it is so important to keep the bigger picture in mind. James, the brother of Jesus, said, *"You are a mist that appears for a little while and then vanishes"* (James 4:14). Not even one half of one percent of people live to be over one hundred years. One hundred years, when compared to eternity, is a drop in the bucket.

When studying difficult things, looking at them from the greater perspective of Jesus is helpful. I try to detach myself and think about it from God's point of view. It is best to try to remove our opinion and see it from the perspective of what the Bible tells us is God's view. In the book of Ephesians, chapter 5, God tells us how husbands and wives should approach each other, and He compares it to Jesus and His bride, which is the Church. When we look at marriage like that and understand that Jesus is married to the Church (which is an unbreakable covenant-love between Jesus and His church), we realize that breaking a marriage covenant should never be taken lightly. It is a serious and somber decision that has spiritual ramifications.

In Matthew 28:20, Jesus promised us that He would *"be with you always, to the very end of the age."* Jesus knows we will sin and fall short of His desires for us. He knows not a single one of us will remain pure and sinless for Him. Yet He promises us that He will never leave us or forsake us. Jesus will be with us no matter what to the very end.

³ Some Pharisees came to him to test him. They asked, "Is it lawful for a man to divorce his wife for any and every reason?" They wanted to know what Jesus would say about this because it was a point of disagreement within society. I know you may disagree with this chapter. This chapter took me almost three weeks to complete because I labored over it and studied for so long. This was a complex and hot topic in Jesus' day and remains much the same today.

Jesus answered them. *⁴ "Haven't you read," he replied, "that at the beginning the Creator 'made them male and female.'"* We won't go deep into this now because we will be hard pressed to make it through this one topic, but Jesus clearly says He created men and women. He does not say we get to define that or change it. We were created a certain way. I know our culture says that it is a choice. However, if we are going to say we are followers of Jesus, we need to listen to His words and let His words define our lives, not our personal lifestyle preferences or what our culture says or teaches.

Jesus continued with the teaching on marriage *⁵ and said, "'For this reason a man will leave his father and mother and be united to his wife, and the two will become one flesh'? ⁶ So they are no longer two, but one flesh. Therefore, what God has joined together, let no one separate."* He told these men that He did not settle for or accept the divorce provision of Deuteronomy 24:1-4. (You may want to study that later.)

Jesus said anyone can read the same Old Testament—the Word of God—that He read growing up. Read from Genesis and see that God created man and woman on day six. Read that God joined man and woman together. Read that God is the one who brings together only two in marriage. Understand that God wants death alone to be what separates a husband and wife. This is why in the traditional and biblical marriage vows, you find only one limitation: "til death do us part" or "as long as you both shall live."

These men followed up with a solid question: *⁷ "Why then," they asked, "did Moses command that a man give his wife a certificate of divorce and send her away?"* This valid question points to how they had been approaching divorce for thousands of years. *⁸ Jesus replied, "Moses permitted you to divorce your wives because your hearts were hard. But it was not this way from the beginning."* Jesus said that Moses allowed it because their hardened hearts wanted it, but it was not how God designed it to be. Nevertheless, here we are again with the hardened hearts of man in conflict with God's perfect plan. God never wanted half the marriages in America to end through divorce, yet that is the average rate of divorce in our current society.

Jesus continued: *⁹ "I tell you that anyone who divorces his wife, except for sexual immorality, and marries another woman commits adultery."* Jesus said that divorce was permitted for sexual immorality and adultery, but He was not mandating it or encouraging it. God always has a greater desire for reconciliation and forgiveness. You can divorce if your spouse keeps slipping back into adultery, but God's desire is always restoration. Look in a reputable study Bible, and there will be a notation that will say something like this: "If adultery breaks the one-flesh uniqueness designed in marriage, divorce and remarriage are possible though never ideal."

Divorce Question #1: If a person divorces for adultery, can they remarry?

Many pastors will refer to Matthew 19 and say you can remarry if there has been adultery and the editors of the study Bible we give away at our church agree. Let's read the passage in Matthew one more time: *⁹"I tell you that anyone who divorces his wife, except for sexual immorality, and marries another woman commits adultery."* Most scholars say that the words "except for sexual immorality" means that if there has been adultery, the aggrieved spouse is free to divorce and remarry.

However, perhaps the greater perspective of not remarrying could be even more critical to our Christian witness. Paul and Jesus are of one mind in that followers of Jesus are radically devoted to one husband and wife as long as they live. This ideal tells the gospel truth: Jesus died for His bride and would never forsake her for another. We should never forsake our spouse, even if they have forsaken us. Even if they sin against us in the worst way, yes, we can divorce them. However, if we remarry, we are never able to be fully restored by the grace of God. God isn't going to call you to leave your second spouse to remarry the first you left. However, if you remain single and God works in both of your lives, it is possible; and when that happens, it is an amazing testimony.

Jesus never forsakes us, never gives up on us, and never wants us to give up on our marriages as long as the other person is living. The vast majority of Scripture teaches us the value of reconciling with all the people who make up the church, which is Jesus' bride. He will never leave us, and we should view our marriages from the perspective of Jesus, not culture.

Divorce Question #2: If a person divorced for a non-Biblical reason and remarried, should he or she leave the later marriage?

If a person divorces for a non-Biblical reason and remarries, but later realizes it was wrong, they should not then divorce their new spouse. What was done is done. Vows have been made, and a new union has happened. Remember, only the sacrifice of Jesus can make things pure. Any couple who repents and seeks God's forgiveness and receives Him is forgiven.

Deuteronomy 24:1-4, where the permission for divorce was given in the law of Moses, speaks of the divorced woman being "defiled" in the second marriage. Then it would be an abomination for her to return to her first husband, even if her second husband died. This language means the second marriage stood, even if it was not God's design.

Secondly, we can look at Jesus' interactions with the woman at the well in John 4. Jesus said to her, *"You have had five husbands, and the man you now have is not your husband"* (John 4:18). When Jesus said, *"The man you have now is not your husband,"* He seems to imply that the other five were her husbands. Not that it's right to divorce and marry five times, but the way Jesus speaks of it sounds like He saw them as real marriages. It is not His design, but it is valid all the same.

A third reason this aligns with Scripture is that there are passages in the Bible that speak of vows being made that should not have been made but were to be kept, such as Joshua's vow to the Gibeonites in Joshua 9. God puts a very high value on keeping our word, even when it should not have been made in the first place. Even if we should not have divorced or remarried for the reasons we did, it is best to keep those new vows rather than to break them. Through Jesus' forgiveness and reconciliation with Him, our first goal has always been godly marriages that are holy before God, in which forgiven, justified husbands and wives desire to live godly lives.

Divorce Question #3: Does death end a marriage in such a way that it is legitimate for a spouse to remarry?

In Romans 7, Paul addresses this question: *¹ Do you not know, brothers and sisters—for I am speaking to those who know the law—that the law has authority over someone only as long as that person lives? ² For example, by law a married woman is bound to her husband as long as he is alive, but if her husband dies, she is released from the law that binds her to him. ³ So then, if she has sexual relations with another man while her husband is still alive, she is called an adulteress. But if her husband dies, she is released from that law and is not an adulteress if she marries another man.*

The answer God gave was yes, it is okay to remarry after the death of a spouse. It is important to also note what Paul says very clearly, which is like what Jesus said in Matthew, that divorcing and remarrying while your spouse is living is not okay. When it comes to adultery and after the death of a spouse, it is always okay. I think the reason for this is that Jesus made plain that in the resurrection, there is no marriage. Matthew 22:30: *³⁰ "At the resurrection people will neither marry nor be given in marriage; they will be like the angels in heaven."*

I have no idea how everything works in heaven. No one does. Based on Jesus' words, if a person said it was wrong to remarry after the death of a spouse, it would seem to imply that marriage is meant to be valid beyond death and in the resurrection. Jesus said it is not. Death is the eternal end of marriage. I will be honest, I do not like that because Jenny has been my love since 8th grade. We have been together for far more of our lives than apart, and I cannot imagine life without her as my partner. However, just because I do not like that does not mean I can change it.

I know a chapter like this hits people in very different ways. I do not share this to condemn or make anyone feel inadequate about their past choices. I share this because it is in the Bible and I believe in teaching the whole counsel of Scripture even when it does not fit our lifestyle. I do not get to cherry-pick the parts of Jesus' life that I like and skip the parts I do not like. If I did, I would not be faithful to teaching as God instructs.

 LIFE APPLICATION

- What is your view of marriage and divorce? Does anything need to change to align with God's view?
- In today's reading, what did you learn about God, yourself, and mankind?
- As a result of today's reading, how will you apply what you learned? Answer as I will…

CHAPTER 61

THE KINGDOM OF GOD IS LIKE

 Matthew 20, Mark 10:32-52, Luke 18:31-43

Confusion comes easily into our culture. There are as many opinions as there are people. There is no difference regarding who the real Jesus was and is. There are many opinions about what Jesus did, taught, and stood for. People love to put their words into His mouth and change what Jesus said about Himself in the Bible as well as what He said about how we should live our lives. The Bible is the only source of perfect truth. Regardless of the topic, the Bible leads us to **the real** answer. In Matthew 20, Jesus told us what the Kingdom of God is like. If you have ever wondered about it, this chapter is for you.

 Matthew 20:1-16

Anyone working for any length of time can relate to this parable of Jesus. When I first graduated from college, I felt like I worked much harder than my boss and was vastly underpaid. We all know people who, in our not-so-humble opinion, neither earned nor deserved what they received. It is clear to us that they didn't deserve a promotion, raise, recognition, or success as much as we did or someone we loved did. We felt like we worked longer and tried harder and yet it seemed to make no difference. Often, we view the world, ourselves, and others through the lens of fairness rather than through the lens of God, which is full of **grace** and **generosity**. Remember, Jesus was teaching what the Kingdom of heaven is like, and the Kingdom of heaven does not look like the world we currently live in.

Our culture has gone overboard with the idea that "everyone is equal" and that "everything has to be fair." God does not see things that way at all. Everyone is not equal or the same, different cultures are not equal or inherently good, and not everything is fair. This is why it is difficult to attend my kid's sporting events, where everyone wins. I have heard my kids cry this inequality out at the dinner table when one gets more broccoli than the others, or when they notice I put all mine on their plates. That was the exact problem Jesus was talking about in this passage. People were getting exactly what they signed up for, but because others were blessed with more, what they were happy with a moment ago was no longer enough.

It isn't just children who desire fairness; adults want it, too. Adults like fairness because it assures us of order, predictability, and control. Fairness is subjectively based on what we think we deserve and reflective of how hard we think we've worked or what we think we've achieved. We live in a wage-based society where we receive what the boss says we earned. The more hours we work, the more sales we make, and the more new customers we bring in, the more money we will receive. If you are a salaried employee and work hard, your chances of promotion are better. This way of thinking exists everywhere in our culture, and it did in Jesus' culture as well. This leads to a question: **What happens when divine goodness trumps human fairness?**

The parable you read suggests wages, earnings, monetary value; all stand in opposition to grace. They are opposing world views. If you read this parable and you really struggled with it, you likely have a wage-based worldview. If you read it and you thought it was awesome, you likely have a grace-based worldview. A wage-based worldview allows little room for grace in our own lives and far less in the lives of others. Grace is dangerous. It reverses business as usual. It is unpredictable. It does not allow us to live neat, orderly lives. It does not let us predict outcomes. Grace is messy.

Look at the words Jesus ended with: [16] *"So the last will be first, and the first will be last."* That's not how a wage-based society works. Here is the strange part of our culture in which every child must win. We see it as fair because it makes everyone feel good, but that is not a Biblical teaching. I can show you that even those who champion this concept in our culture do NOT truly believe in it.

I would bet that none of those who think every child should be affirmed through equal ribbons and trophies would agree with the following scenario. Imagine they are hired to work at a company the same day as their neighbor. They have the same job and boss, and both work 40 hours a week. I am sure that person would be fine with equal pay, unless they end up working 60 hours a week while their neighbor only puts in 20 hours a week… but with the same wage. I doubt they would be okay with that. Even in our culture, we are not fully vested in an "all is equal system" if that unfairness targets our children or us.

Wages reveal human effort and efficiency and make distinctions and separations based on merit or popularity. Grace is totally different. Grace looks beyond our productivity, appearance, ethnicity, accomplishments, or failures. Grace recognizes there is more to you than what you have done or left undone. Grace reveals the goodness of God. Grace is not based on anything we do or do not do; it is based 100% on God's choice, which is why it is so hard for us to accept. Wage-based lifestyles are all about what we do or do not do, who we know or do not know, where we work, where we live, how we invest, and so on. On the other hand, **a grace-based life asks us to show up and open up to receive what God is giving.** When we do, we see our lives, the world, and neighbors differently.

This reminds me of a story of a friend of mine who is a lawyer. In some law firms, like many sales teams, a score sheet is distributed to everyone every month. A law firm lists the name of every attorney, the number of hours they worked, the number of hours billed, and the number of dollars collected. It gives the basis for wages and bonuses. It gives incentive for comparison, competition, expectation, and judgments. You know who began work at dawn, who slept in until 9 a.m., who took the extra-long lunch break, who took off early at 4 p.m., etc.

I would guess many of you find yourself judging others who do not meet your unspoken expectations. Grace reminds us that we are not as self-sufficient as we pretend to be. Grace shows us that our worth is not determined by our productivity or usefulness to our company. Grace does not justify or excuse. Grace is not worried about what is fair. On the contrary, grace holds before us the truth that every person is more than their behavior, looks, accomplishments, or failures.

The tragedy of a wage-based life is that it blinds us to the presence of grace in our own lives and the lives of others. Having a wage-based mentality can make us resent grace, despise goodness, and hate generosity because we want it for ourselves instead of others. **Wage-based mentality makes life all about us.** Wage-based living separates and isolates us from others. Eventually, besides setting standards and expectations for ourselves and others, we, sadly, also set them for God. That is exactly what we see in this parable.

Let's read this again. *¹ "For the kingdom of heaven is like a landowner who went out early in the morning to hire workers for his vineyard."* Remember, this story was not about these men but about how things work in the Kingdom of God. God is the landlord who *² "agreed to pay them a denarius for the day and sent them into his vineyard."* The workers were okay with this wage because a denarius was a fair wage for one day of work. This wage would have been the same as being paid minimum wage for manual labor.

³ "About nine in the morning he went out and saw others standing in the marketplace doing nothing. ⁴ He told them, 'You also go and work in my vineyard, and I will pay you whatever is right.' ⁵ So they went."

This is the same thing that happened at the local paint store when I was a builder. I would pick up as many guys as I needed, and they jumped in my truck. I took them to the job site, and they worked for a fair wage.

⁵ "He went out again about noon and about three in the afternoon and did the same thing. ⁶ About five in the afternoon he went out and found still others standing around. He asked them, 'Why have you been standing here all day long doing nothing?' ⁷ "'Because no one has hired us,' they answered. "He said to them, 'You also go and work in my vineyard.'" Remember that this is not about picking up guys at the paint store. This is about the kingdom of God. God keeps going back and looking for people and seeking people. Never forget that God never gives up on reaching us.

⁸ "When evening came, the owner of the vineyard said to his foreman, 'Call the workers and pay them their wages, beginning with the last ones hired and going on to the first.'" If God had paid these guys the opposite way, the problem would not have come up because when you get paid, you leave. God wanted them to see this, so He reversed the regular order of paying the men.

⁹ "The workers who were hired about five in the afternoon came and each received a denarius." In our culture, that would mean they worked for about an hour, so they *earned* one hour of minimum wage but received a full day's pay. Great deal for those guys, for sure! If I were one of the first workers, I would expect to get seven times more because I worked seven times longer than the others.

¹⁰ "So when those came who were hired first, they expected to receive more. But each one of them also received a denarius. They all received the same wage. ¹¹ When they received it, they began to grumble against the landowner." Just like most of us would. So, the workers said, *¹² "'These who were hired last worked only one hour,' they said, 'and you have made them equal to us who have borne the burden of the work and the heat of the day.'"* Can you hear them? "This isn't fair! They didn't work as hard as we did!" So, here is a good question to ponder: **What is your reaction when something *unfair* happens to you?**

They saw themselves as different and more deserving than those hired later. They grumbled against the generosity of the business owner. Neither set of workers owned the vineyard. All of those people needed a job. They were all invited by no effort of their own. They were just standing around town and doing nothing.

However, there is something that distinguishes the first hired and the last hired. The distinction is not what time they showed up to work. The fundamental distinction between the first people hired and all the people hired later was the terms under which they entered the vineyard to work. The first group entered the vineyard only after agreeing to what was good enough and normal; a full day's work for a full day's pay. That is what happens in a wage-based society. We settle for good enough because we like to play it safe, even when God has a better plan for us.

The first-hired men received what they agreed to and what the culture said was normal. The later-hired workers, who came at 9 a.m., Noon, 3 p.m., and 5 p.m., did not negotiate for the usual daily wage. Did you pick up on that? Go back and reread this section. The men entered the vineyard trusting they would be paid [4] *"whatever is right."* Whatever was right was not determined by the first-hired worker or society. Whatever was right was determined by the goodness and grace of the owner.

The later-hired workers received more than they earned, more than they deserved, and more than they had a right to ask or hope for. That is what God does: [4] *"whatever is right"* isn't about fairness; it is about grace. Why settle for the usual when God wants to give you [4] *"whatever is right"* for your life? Why settle for meeting your needs when God wants to bless you more than you can imagine? Why settle for "enough for today" when God tells us He will give us more than our barns could ever store?

If we are honest, most of us prefer a wage-based life because we prefer predictability more than anything else. However, if you want to step out of this wage-based mentality, which makes life all about us, you need to make a radical change. You need to understand: **A grace-based mentality makes life all about God.**

No more comparing your life to your siblings, your house to your friend's house, or your stuff to your neighbor's stuff. Refuse to compete in such a way that someone must lose for you to win. Trust that, in God's world, there is enough for everyone. Let go of expectations based on what you think you or others deserve. Give God the freedom to give whatever is right to everyone. Know that God's ways are not your ways (Isaiah 55:8). Decide today you are no longer the judge in life; the judge is God alone. That is the way of grace, the way of God.

 LIFE APPLICATION

- How different will your life look if you let go of comparison, competition, expectation, and judgment? How can you praise God when He blesses another instead of being jealous?
- In today's reading, what did you learn about God, yourself, and mankind?
- As a result of today's reading, how will you apply what you learned? Answer as I will…

CHAPTER 62

TRIUMPHAL ENTRY

 John 11:55-12:1 & 9-19, Luke 19:36-46

When I was younger, I worked as a teen zookeeper at Potter Park Zoo in Lansing, Michigan. I loved helping the zookeepers feed the wild animals. On the fourth of July, the female burro gave birth to a male, whom they named Firecracker. The father didn't like having another male in the enclosure and was constantly biting his son. It got so bad that they decided they would need to find another zoo for the baby. I told them my family would take him. Shockingly, my dad agreed to let me have the baby burro. We built a small barn, put up a fence, and went to pick him up on a Saturday. He was so small that we were able to take him home in my mom's minivan. We renamed him Tinker, and he was a pretty cool pet. Later, we bought him a girlfriend because we did not want him to be lonely. When I was older, I noticed Tinker and Belle (his girlfriend) had curious markings on their backs. I will get back to this in a minute, but first, let's read the passage.

 John 11:55-57, John 12:1 & 9-11

Jewish men were required to go to Jerusalem for the festival you read about. The leaders of the Jewish faith knew that Jesus would be coming. They let everyone know that if anyone saw Jesus, they should report it so the leaders could arrest Him. This was a scare tactic to try to discredit Jesus. This was because His movement was still experiencing explosive growth, which the religious leaders hated. Bear in mind that before Jesus got there for this festival, the opposition had tried to do everything possible to dissuade people from having anything to do with Him.

Remember when Jesus raised his friend Lazarus from the

dead a few chapters ago? Well, that significantly impacted the community, as anyone would expect. However, the religious leaders did not appreciate how it led people away from their leadership. Just like how we do not like it when a good employee goes to another company or when our favorite player takes a deal with another team. It can lead us to feel like they did in this passage: *¹⁰ So the chief priests made plans to kill Lazarus as well, ¹¹ for on account of him many of the Jews were going over to Jesus and believing in him.*

When Jesus raised Lazarus from the dead, this created a massive problem for the religious leaders. They had to figure out how they could discredit Jesus, even though they all knew He performed a miracle by raising Lazarus from the dead. People came to believe in Jesus in droves because they realized He had authority and power that the other religious leaders did not.

 John 12:12-19

Let's go back to the markings on my donkeys. There is a cool legend about the donkey's cross. Legend says that the donkey that carried Jesus into Jerusalem on Palm Sunday followed Him to Calvary. Appalled by the sight of Jesus on the cross, the donkey turned away but could not leave. It is said that the shadow of the cross fell upon the shoulders and back of the donkey. Due to the donkey's faithfulness to Jesus, people can see a cross-marking on all donkeys. This is a testimony of the love and devotion of a humble, little donkey. While this is simply a legend, I love it because my two donkeys indeed had a cross on their back.

The story of Jesus riding on a donkey wasn't something that happened by chance, but was prophesied more than 500 years before the birth of Jesus. The prophet Zechariah wrote in Zechariah 9:9, *Rejoice greatly, Daughter Zion! Shout, Daughter*

Jerusalem! See, your king comes to you, righteous and victorious, lowly and riding on a donkey, on a colt, the foal of a donkey.

Isaiah prophesied about this event around 740 B.C., almost 800 years before it happened. Isaiah 62:11 reads, *The LORD has made proclamation to the ends of the earth: "Say to Daughter Zion, 'See, your Savior comes! See, his reward is with him, and his recompense accompanies him.'"* The Old Testament, or the first part of the Bible, was written hundreds of years before Jesus' birth, and contains over 300 prophecies that Jesus fulfilled through His life, death, and resurrection.

Here are some very logical facts for you to ponder. Mathematically speaking, the odds of anyone fulfilling as many prophecies as Jesus did is staggering. Mathematicians put it this way:
- One person fulfilling eight prophecies has the odds of 1 in 100,000,000,000,000,000.
- One person fulfilling 48 prophecies has the odds of 1 in 10… to the 157th power!
- One person fulfilling 300+ prophecies (as Jesus did) is mathematically impossible or miraculous.

That is pure factual math. Here is the definition of a **miracle** or miraculous event: **a surprising and welcome event that is not explicable by natural or scientific laws and is therefore considered to be the work of a divine agency.**

The magnificent detail of these prophecies marks the Bible as the inspired Word of God. Only God has foreknowledge and could accomplish all that was written about Jesus. The historical accuracy and reliability set the Bible apart from any other book or record in all of history. This is important because it sheds light on why *¹⁶ At first his disciples did not understand all this.*

When you are amid great things happening, you often cannot see them. Some of you do not see the amazing ways Jesus is moving right now. One day you will look back and be able to and see it. *¹⁶ Only after Jesus was glorified did they realize that these things had been written about him and that these things had been done to him. ¹⁷ Now the crowd that was with him when he called Lazarus from the tomb and raised him from the dead continued to spread the word. ¹⁸ Many people, because they had heard that he had performed this sign, went out to meet him. ¹⁹ So the Pharisees said to one another, "See, this is getting us nowhere. Look how the whole world has gone after him!"*

You know far more about Jesus than these people did. These people had no idea that soon Jesus was going to raise Himself from the dead and prove He was God. Even without that knowledge, as verse 17 says, they spread the word about what Jesus was doing.

What are you doing to spread the good news of Jesus? Do you talk to your friends, neighbors, coworkers, and family members who do not know Jesus? Here is the point: **People who genuinely believe in Jesus tell others about Jesus.**

There is no category for a true believer in Jesus who does not share Jesus. If that offends you, I encourage you to search for one place in the Bible that tells us we are not called to share the good news of Jesus. If you want to save time, you will not find a place because there is not one.

 Luke 19:36-46

Luke continued the story, telling us the Pharisees were telling Jesus, *³⁹ "Teacher, rebuke your disciples!"* They wanted the disciples to stop saying Jesus was the Messiah they were looking for. They did not want Jesus to be the King of the Jews because the religious leaders wanted a king who supported their agenda. Jesus did not support their agenda, so naturally they did not like Him. We should be able to relate to this because it is similar to what we see in politics today. If you support a party's agenda, they love you. If you do not support a party's agenda, they will try to destroy you. It was the same way in Jesus' day and age.

By riding into Jerusalem on a donkey and proclaiming to be the Messiah, as written in the prophecies we read earlier, Jesus threw down the glove and responded to the religious leaders. *[40] "I tell you," He replied, "if they keep quiet, the stones will cry out." [41] As he approached Jerusalem and saw the city, he wept over it [42] and said, "If you, even you, had only known on this day what would bring you peace—but now it is hidden from your eyes. [43] The days will come upon you when your enemies will build an embankment against you and encircle you and hem you in on every side. [44] They will dash you to the ground, you and the children within your walls. They will not leave one stone on another, because you did not recognize the time of God's coming to you."* Jesus repeated another prophecy, telling them that one day everything they held near and dear would be destroyed because they had denied who Jesus was.

Even if Jesus fulfilled the 300 prophecies you read about above, Jesus had to get this one right as well. If you study history, you know that He did. In 70 A.D. and 135 A.D., Rome did precisely what Jesus said would happen and attacked and destroyed Jerusalem in this manner. Jesus was not some random guy who did some great stuff once upon a time and was made into a god to make us feel good. There is no way Jesus could say what He said and have done what He did with such perfect accuracy unless He was, is, and will always be God.

The praise lavished on Jesus by the ordinary people was not because they recognized Him as their Savior from sin. They welcomed Him out of their desire for a deliverer who would lead them in a revolt against Rome. Many followed Jesus because they hoped He would bring Israel back to power and prominence in the world. These people who hailed Him as King with their praises in this story are the same people who will soon call for Jesus' death when He fails to meet their expectations. Those who hailed Him as a hero will soon reject and abandon Him.

The story of the triumphal entry is one of contrasts, and those contrasts contain applications to all believers. It is the story of the king who came as a lowly servant on a donkey, not a prancing stallion, or in royal robes or with a royal entourage. He was a king who wore the clothes of the poor and common people. He was a humble leader. Jesus came not to conquer by force as earthly kings do. He came to show love, grace, and mercy and to sacrifice Himself for His people. It was not a kingdom of armies, splendor, and power but a kingdom of lowliness and servanthood. He came not to conquer nations but to heal and change hearts and minds. His message was one of peace, not with other countries but with God.

If Jesus has made a triumphal entry into our hearts, He reigns there in peace and love. As His followers, we exhibit those same qualities, and the world sees the true King living and reigning in triumph within us. Plenty of people "follow" Jesus today because they want Jesus to do things for them just as these people did. However, believing in Jesus is not about what you get from Him. It is about truly giving all of yourself to Jesus.

 LIFE APPLICATION

- Are you following Jesus because you want something from Him (salvation, help, a good life, etc.)? Or are you following Jesus because you want to give Him 100% of you (life, wealth, career, love)?
- In today's reading, what did you learn about God, yourself, and mankind?
- As a result of today's reading, how will you apply what you learned? Answer as I will…

CHAPTER 63

JESUS' SECOND CLEANSING OF THE TEMPLE

 Luke 19:45-48, Mark 11:15-18, Matthew 21:12-13

You may remember an earlier chapter where Jesus cleansed the temple. I don't think it is coincidental that Jesus did this both at the start and then toward the end of His ministry.

Let me ask you two questions: Have you ever struggled with anger? Is anger a sin? It may surprise you, but anger is not necessarily a sin. Anger cannot always be sinful because, at times, God is angry. So, the question is this: when is anger righteous instead of sinful?

When we study the Bible and read about God's anger, it always stems from unholiness. God gets angry when people behave in ungodly ways. What you are about to read happened to people who should have known better. Yet, they acted in a way that brought dishonor to God the Father, so Jesus was indeed angry.

 Luke 19:45-48

When I think about this passage, it makes me smile because of what we see Jesus do. It causes me to smile because I think about people today looking for a reason to never attend church. If Jesus came to your local church and acted like this, I bet the crowd would be much smaller the next Sunday. The problem is that many of us do not want to see who we really are. We don't like to be called out when we behave badly. That makes us, at times, not want to see Jesus for who He really is either.

Don't miss what was happening in this passage. These are people who have spent their entire lives in their version of church.

They are people who spent their lives behaving in a way they believed was not only okay but good. Now Jesus is demanding that they stop doing something that was right to them.

The religious people missed the point again. *⁴⁵ When Jesus entered the temple courts, he began to drive out those who were selling.* Mark 11 says He flipped over tables. If you remember the last time, He made a whip and went after people. I want to draw you back to what I said in our last chapter on this topic because for most of us, our picture of Jesus was a slender, white, good-looking man. Let me remind you that we have no idea what Jesus looked like. The Bible said that He was not handsome and there was nothing on the outside to attract people to Him. Jesus would have looked like a Middle Eastern man who, because of His job as a carpenter (or stone mason), would have had a serious set of muscles.

The Hebraic scholar James W. Fleming said, "Jesus and Joseph would have formed and made nine out of ten projects from stone either by chiseling or carving the stone by hand or stacking building blocks." Another reason why it is most likely that Jesus and Joseph worked with stone was that Nazareth was only three miles from the ancient town of Zippori. During the first century, Zippori developed rapidly under the reign of Herod Antipas and eventually became "the jewel of all Galilee" by Jewish historian Josephus. Herod's massive beautification project would have required the help of every available and skilled carpenter in the surrounding area, likely including Joseph. Joseph and Jesus would have been in the perfect location to commute to work, for halfway between Nazareth and Zippori was an enormous rock quarry.

This makes more sense as to the reason Jesus refers to Himself in this way: *"The stone the builders rejected has become the cornerstone."* (Luke 20:17), or how He would be the "cornerstone," and why Peter called us to be living stones (1 Peter 2).

Reread this: *⁴⁵ When Jesus entered the temple courts, he began to drive out those who were selling.* God demanded in the Old Testament that people make sacrifices based on the kinds of sins they committed. That was how the system worked. It was God's system and He put it into place. Jesus was not angry with the people there in obedience to God's system. The problem wasn't selling someone the necessary sacrificial animals. The problem was the people who were "changing money."

The temple leaders decided that Gentile money could not be used at the temple because of the graven images stamped on it by Rome. So, the temple leaders decided to make a currency for the temple. Then they set their exchange rate, thereby enabling them to exploit people coming to them to help them get right with God. The priests found a way to skim extra money for themselves from the Jewish people's obedience to God. The righteous anger of Jesus makes more sense when we know the reason behind it. Over time, the church leaders allowed their hearts and purpose to become corrupt, and they allowed corruption to creep into God's house.

This happens in our lives. We think we can watch this TV show or that movie, drink this, smoke that, say this or gossip about that, buy this or charge that, all because it doesn't hurt anyone. Yet over time, you look back at this mountain of debt, addiction, or wrongdoing and wonder where it came from. **Things can start with a good purpose, but minor adjustments can lead us astray over time if we are not careful.**

You may be reading this thinking that it is the story of you, your marriage, or your family. There is still hope! If you allow God to refocus your marriage, your family, or yourself, things can change! Think about your greatest passion in life. It could be anything from sewing to football, from God to golf. Perhaps it is your kids, grandkids, career, spouse, or someone you love and would do anything for. What are you most zealous or passionate about? What does everyone know you are the biggest fan of? What does everyone who truly knows you say you are obsessed with? What consumes you? Answer this:

Am I willing to be as zealous for God as I am for _____ (write in your greatest passion).

Now contrast your greatest passion to what Jesus was passionate about. [46] *"It is written," he said to them, "'My house will be a house of prayer'; but you have made it 'a den of robbers.'"* Jesus was passionate about His Father's house because His Father's house was a place where people prayed to connect with God. If someone were abusing or distorting the design of God's house, would you care?

Place yourself in this scene with Jesus. Imagine the chaos of the temple courts when cows, sheep, and other animals suddenly ran all over, trampled over people and broke things as they tried to flee. Can you imagine seeing Jesus turn His attention to the money changers sitting behind those tables and the shock on their faces as He sent money flying? Fear and chaos ensued, and at that moment, everyone realized they had better get out of there. Jesus didn't stop at the money changers; He moved toward the people selling birds and yelled at them, "Get out of here!"

Imagine the shock of being Jesus' disciples at that moment. I can hear them saying to one another, "Should we stop Jesus and talk Him down off the ledge?" Maybe they were in shock that this was happening again. Just when it seemed like everything was going great for Jesus, He did this. The Bible says Jesus drove them out and then [47] *Every day he was teaching at the temple.*

Jesus showed everyone what the purpose of the temple, or church, truly is: teaching people about God and leading people toward God. I am sure you figured out that this was not going to sit well with the religious leaders who didn't like Him, and you are right. *⁴⁷ But the chief priests, the teachers of the law and the leaders among the people were trying to kill him. ⁴⁸ Yet they could not find any way to do it, because all the people hung on his words.*

They wanted Jesus eliminated because they could not control or stop Him. Most of all, they wanted Jesus killed because the people were starting to follow Him and not them. We know Jesus grew up loving the temple and loving the house of God. You might remember that when He was a young boy at the temple, He got so caught up that His family mistakenly left Him behind. Jesus loved being in the house of God so much! No wonder that when He came back at 30 years of age and when He saw what was really going on, it tore Him apart. He couldn't let it go on. It is no wonder that His heart was deeply grieved by the fact that, after three years of His teaching, these people who should have known better were still missing the point. You are three books into the life of Jesus. Have you grasped how all this applies to your life yet?

LIFE APPLICATION

- Write down the things you are most passionate about. What consumes most of your time, where do you invest most of your talent, where do you spend most of your treasure? Ponder how you could add more godly things on your list.
- In today's reading, what did God teach you about God, yourself, and mankind?
- As a result of today's reading, how will you apply what you learned? Answer as, I will…

CHAPTER 64

JESUS PREDICTS HIS DEATH

 John 12:20-50

While working on this chapter, I was in Argentina hunting with a group of guys from Family Church. I always dreamed of hunting a red stag from the time I first saw a mount of one at a hunting show. At that show, I asked a guy named Lon if they were real or if it was a fake mount because it looked like something out of the movie *The Lord of the Rings*. One of the things that I do when I am hunting is to envision the perfect animal walking right out in front of me. Then I envision how I would help it go meet Jesus (well, maybe not because I don't know that all animals go to heaven). I have realized that things rarely go as I envision them. Jesus, on the other hand, told us how His life would end, and He was spot on.

 John 12:20-50

It is fascinating that this passage begins with Greek men from a non-religious background coming to speak with Jesus. Philip and Andrew told Jesus that these Greeks want to "see Him." Jesus' response is odd: *²³ "The hour has not come for the Son of Man to be glorified."* His disciples had no idea that Jesus was talking about His coming death and resurrection. That is why Jesus continued saying, *²⁴ "Very truly I tell you, unless a kernel of wheat falls to the ground and dies, it remains only a single seed. But if it dies, it produces many seeds."* Jesus wanted them to know that the pathway to glory is for everyone, including the Greeks who wanted to see Him, through His death. Jesus taught them that they would see the glory of God and the fruit of God's plan. It would happen first through Jesus' death, then as His disciples took those seeds of the good news of Jesus' resurrection to all people, and lastly to each succeeding generation... all the way to you and me.

Jesus explained that His plan would be the same for those who followed Him! Jesus would die for our salvation, and His desire was for His followers to commit to a life of sacrifice for others like He did. To see Jesus, you must prepare to become like Him. Prepare to follow Him on the road He took. This was hard to understand back then and still is today.

Jesus followed up with this: *[25] "Anyone who loves their life will lose it, while anyone who hates their life in this world will keep it for eternal life. [26] Whoever serves me must follow me; and where I am, my servant also will be. My Father will honor the one who serves me."*

Here are the hard questions Jesus expects us to answer:

Will we love our lives in this world more than we love Jesus?

Will we follow Jesus no matter where He leads us?

Will we serve like Jesus did, no matter the personal cost to us?

Will we let the truth about Jesus define our lives?

Take some time to think about those questions. Realize that none of these people knew the end of the story. None of them had experienced the last days of Jesus or His resurrection. You are somewhere in the world reading this with greater knowledge than they had. What are you doing to align with Jesus? If you align with Jesus by imitating Him, you will show Jesus to the world and become like Jesus so that others may see Him through your life. You will find that **becoming like Jesus is hard and glorious!**

You won't want to miss the hard or the glorious. If you focus on the hard parts of life but give up because hard things are challenging, you will miss the glorious part yet to come. Never give up! In the same way, if you only see the glorious part, you will minimize the sacrifices you made to find the glorious. Ask yourself: **Is my focus balanced and honest? Is there anything that must die within me to regain a balanced perspective?**

What habit or issue might need to die in you to bear more fruit for God? It's a scary question—personally and corporately. I know this sounds odd, so I want to spend some time here. Becoming a real Christian means we let go of or put to death our old self. Then we take on a newness of life by our faith in Jesus! Paul put it like this in Galatians 2:20: *I have been crucified with Christ and I no longer live, but Christ lives in me. The life I now live in the body, I live by faith in the Son of God, who loved me and gave himself for me.*

When we talk about dying to self, it truly means becoming more like Jesus and less like us. It is good to ask God what in me must die so that I might be a more fruitful father, wife, business owner, student, and so forth. It is good to ask God to reveal that to you. This even applies in other areas of your life. Ask, "What in me must die in my business, church, school, etc. for me to be more fruitful and reach more people for Jesus?"

Next, we read, *²⁷ "Now my soul is troubled, and what shall I say? 'Father, save me from this hour'? No, it was for this very reason I came to this hour. ²⁸ Father, glorify your name!"* Imagine knowing your brutal death was coming but still saying, "Father, God, Dad, do not rescue me from a brutal death because I want Your glory shown more than I want to be spared from what is coming." Incredible! The disciples still had no idea what Jesus was inferring. Jesus kept saying the same thing in different ways, hoping that it would connect and that they would remember what He had said when all of it happened before their eyes.

Read verse 37 and take a minute to let it sink in. *³⁷ Even after Jesus had done all these miraculous signs in their presence, they would still not believe in him.*

Do you think it would be easier to believe in Jesus or talk to people about Jesus if you saw Him do miracles? I have heard that a lot from people. I have also heard people say that if they could see God, or if God spoke to them directly, then they would believe. That was the same thing the disciples thought and felt when Jesus was with them. We still struggle with the same things they did thousands of years ago. We choose not to see God. We have the Bible, yet we choose not to believe it. We know so much more about Jesus than these people did, but we choose not to believe because something Jesus said does not align with our preferred way of living. We are the same today. Unbelief is nothing new.

John wrote that the prophet Isaiah, who lived generations before Jesus, said unbelief will happen. *³⁸ This was to fulfill the word of Isaiah the prophet: "Lord, who has believed our message and to whom has the arm of the Lord been revealed?" ³⁹ For this reason they could not believe, because, as Isaiah says elsewhere: ⁴⁰ "He has blinded their eyes and hardened their hearts, so they can neither see with their eyes, nor understand with their hearts, nor turn—and I would heal them." ⁴¹ Isaiah said this because he saw Jesus' glory and spoke about him. ⁴² Yet at the same time many even among the leaders believed in him. But because of the Pharisees they would not openly acknowledge their faith for fear they would be put out of the synagogue; ⁴³ for they loved human praise more than praise from God.*

Here is a modern-day translation of the passage above. "But because of their boss, they would not openly acknowledge their faith for fear of being fired. But because of their spouse, they would not openly acknowledge their faith for fear of being ridiculed. But because of their boyfriend or girlfriend, they would not openly acknowledge their faith for fear of breaking up. But because of their coach or friends, they would not openly acknowledge their faith for fear of being made fun of. For they loved the praise of other people more than God."

When I was in school, I hated history and thought it was a waste of time. Then I grew up and realized that history does repeat itself. As I grew older, I realized that we continue to fall into the same traps that people did thousands of years ago. I began to wonder why we don't learn from our ancestors. I have no answer, other than for some reason, as we age, our repeated mistakes become obvious.

⁴⁴ Then Jesus cried out, "Whoever believes in me does not believe in me only, but in the one who sent me. ⁴⁵ The one who looks at me is seeing the one who sent me." This was the cry of Jesus throughout His ministry. From the beginning to the end, Jesus claimed that He and the Father were one in John 10:30 and again in John 14:9. Both are Scriptures central to the Gospel and our Christian faith. If you don't have Jesus as your Savior, you don't have God as your Father. *"No one who denies the Son has the Father; whoever acknowledges the Son has the Father also"* (1 John 2:23).

What you do with Jesus is the clearest test of what you do with God. Jesus continued, *⁴⁶ "I have come into the world as a light, so that no one who believes in me should stay in darkness."* This was the last time in the Gospel of John that Jesus called Himself the Light of the World, but this name was given to Him from the beginning. John 1:5: *"The light shines in the darkness, and the darkness has not overcome it."* Everyone who receives Jesus moves from the darkness of ignorance to the light of truth and fellowship with God.

Jesus concluded with these words: *⁴⁷ "If anyone hears my words but does not keep them, I do not judge that person. For I did not come to judge the world, but to save the world. ⁴⁸ There is a judge for the one who rejects me and does not accept my words; the very words I have spoken will condemn them at the last day. ⁴⁹ For I did not speak on my own, but the Father who sent me commanded me to say all that I have spoken. ⁵⁰ I know that his command leads to eternal life. So whatever I say is just what the Father has told me to say."*

For two thousand years, we have had exactly what we need—the Words of God. Reading the Bible is how we know God and build a relationship with Him. What would God have you remove from your life to walk closer with Him? Don't be afraid of following where He leads you. Following God can be very scary, but it will be the best decision you ever make!

 **LIFE APPLICATION**

- Is there something God is calling you to put to death so that you might experience Him more fully? Are you striving against your nature as a Christian to keep something that God wants removed? Follow where God leads you and do not fear following His leading!
- In today's reading, what did God teach you about God, yourself, and mankind?
- As a result of today's reading, how will you apply what you learned? Answer as, I will…

_____
_____
_____
_____
_____

CHAPTER 65

BUCKING AUTHORITY

 Matthew 21:23-46, 22:1-7, Mark 11:27-12:12, Luke 20:1-19

Scripture can be brutal at times and can feel like a stab to the heart if you are spiritually sensitive or if you have a sin issue. As I was studying the passage you are about to read, a retired pastor named Charles was painting in my office. I said, "Charles, imagine if I said this to people Sunday morning." I then read him what you are about to read. Charles started laughing, shook his head, and said, "Nice knowing you, pastor." That is just a fair warning to you that what Jesus said in this passage is a bit intense but still true.

 Matthew 21:23-32

This passage reminds me of when political correctness began in America. Cancel culture became so powerful that people could not answer the question, "What is true?" So many people believed they would be trapped by their own words, so they said nothing, like these religious leaders chose to do. The leaders could not answer with the truth, or the opposite of what was true, because then the people would revolt against them. So, they decided to do neither. But if Jesus had tried the same tactic, sparks would have flown. Sound familiar? Watch any political debate and you will see leaders play these same games today. If only we would read and learn from the Bible, imagine how much better our lives would be!

On the heels of this, Jesus told three parables. Quickly, things became intense and a bit funny. *[28] "What do you think? There was a man who had two sons. He went to the first and said, 'Son, go and work today in the vineyard.' [29] "'I will not,' he answered, but later he changed his mind and went*[30] *"Then the father went to the other son and said the same thing. He answered, 'I will, sir,' but he did not go.* [31] *"Which of the two did what his father wanted?" "The first," they answered." Jesus said to them, "Truly I tell you, the tax collectors and the prostitutes are entering the kingdom of God ahead of you."* Can you hear the gasps that would happen as Jesus told that story?

Jesus was quite direct and didn't mince words. Jesus told them that John had come before Him and showed them how to live and that the worst of sinners they could imagine had heard the message, believed, repented, and changed. However, the religious people listened to the SAME message and did NOTHING to change. Thus, the sinners would enter heaven AHEAD of the religious people! The "worst sinners" would go to heaven because they repented and changed their lives. Ouch! Ironic that those who were sure they were aligned with God were also sure they knew who was not in step with God. Unfortunately, they had it all backwards.

That was what I read to Charles that day. He and I both know that if we talked like that, people would be furious with us. The reality is that there are many American Christians in this same boat, people who know a lot about God but who do not apply any of that knowledge to their lives. Too many people know right from wrong, but by their actions, they clearly have no desire to let God rearrange their lives according to His design. Too many people want to live their lives their way, with no regard for God's design, and still claim to be followers of Jesus. News flash! You can do that on earth, but that is an obvious indicator that you are not an authentic follower of Jesus.

Jesus was about to clear up the facts. You cannot cherry-pick how you follow Him. You cannot decide what parts of the Bible you like and live out only those parts. You cannot remove parts of the Bible that do not align with your preferred way of life.

Jesus was not, and is still not, looking for partially committed followers. Jesus, God, and the Holy Spirit are looking for fully devoted followers of Jesus Christ. That is just as relevant today as it was 2,000 years ago. Here is the bottom line: **Performance is what matters. Promises are meaningless.**

Everyone reading this knows that is true. You know who in your family or friend group always promises things and never lives up to the promise. As a result, you don't trust them when you need something important done. You also know those people whom you can depend on in an emergency. We should strive to be people who do not need to promise things because the performance of our lives shows who we are.

The same applies to our walk with Jesus. He does not want to hear promises about how one day we will begin faithfully following Him. He does not want to hear promises of how we will put Him first... one day. Jesus wants to see our actions align with our words. Interestingly, Jesus does not stop there. He intended to drive this point home! As you read the following parable, remember it refers to how people have treated God for generations and how Jesus was treated when He came to earth.

 Matthew 21:33-46

This parable can apply to anyone who has owned something and been cheated by another person. Keep in mind that these parables are to teach about God and ourselves. God is the landowner in this scenario. In verse 35, the people rejected His ownership. In verse 36, He tried again. Just like how over the generations God continually sent prophets, priests, and pastors to try to lead people toward Himself, but they rejected the message. Their rejection even went so far sometimes that they beat, stoned, or killed those people. Lastly, this landowner sent his son. After all, they would surely treat him well, just like God sent Jesus, because surely people would see His life and actions and then believe.

38 "But when the tenants saw the son, they said to each other, 'This is the heir. Come, let's kill him and take his inheritance.' 39 So they took him and threw him out of the vineyard and killed him. 40 "Therefore, when the owner of the vineyard comes, what will he do to those tenants?" 41 "He will bring those wretches to a wretched end," they replied, "and he will rent the vineyard to other tenants, who will give him his share of the crop at harvest time." 42 Jesus said to them, "Have you never read in the Scriptures: "'The stone the builders rejected has become the cornerstone; the Lord has done this, and it is marvelous in our eyes'? 43 "Therefore I tell you that the kingdom of God will be taken away from you and given to a people who will produce its fruit. 44 Anyone who falls on this stone will be broken to pieces; anyone on whom it falls will be crushed."

This certainly offended the religious leaders. Imagine if you were talking to me about your sins, and I said, "Have you ever read the Bible? Because clearly the Bible says the opposite of what your life is showing." Would that offend you?

In our culture, we are taught that offending someone is the worst sin ever. You cannot offend anyone, and if you do, you are accused of being a terrible person. If Jesus offended people, which He did, then causing an offense in and of itself could not be a sin. When you offend someone because you present the truth, it is not a sin. Please do not listen to our culture that tells you to be politically correct on everything. The truth is worth far more than being politically correct. True believers fearlessly proclaim what God says in the Bible because it is the truth. Just because someone might not like the truth does not mean it is untrue and certainly doesn't mean that it should go unspoken.

Don't miss verse 43. It teaches us that if you do not produce fruit—if your life does not reflect what you say you believe—you will not have a spot in the kingdom of God. Your life shows what you really believe. Your life shows where you are heading because **heaven-bound people produce heavenly fruit on earth.** Have you ever thought about what kind of godly fruit you have produced? Have you ever helped a person connect with God? Have you ever helped a person overcome something?

The ending to this parable is filled with irony! *⁴⁵ When the chief priests and the Pharisees heard Jesus' parables, they knew he was talking about them. ⁴⁶ They looked for a way to arrest him, but they were afraid of the crowd because the people held that he was a prophet.* They were offended, so they wanted to find a way to get rid of Jesus. Exactly like in the parable they had just heard, but their ears had been closed to the truth. They no longer recognized the truth. Similar to our politics today, their hands were tied because of the masses and their desire to keep power.

 Matthew 22:1-7

The Parable of the Wedding Banquet refers to what will happen in the book of Revelation (the last book of the Bible). Of course, at that time, they had no idea there would one day be a book of Revelation because it had yet to be written. It begins with a king (God) who sent out invitations for his son's wedding banquet. He sent out his servant to deliver a save-the-date, but those invited refused to answer. The king told his servant to tell them it was ready and time to come! The king did not get the response he hoped for, so he sent a second invitation. You may not understand this because we do not live in a monarchy, but a second invite from a king was not a request. It was not to be ignored. This would be like when you tell your kids to pick up their rooms. The first time, you are nice about it. The second time, you're not so nice. The third time, punishment is coming their way.

The parable tells us, *⁵ "But they paid no attention and went off—one to his field, another to his business. ⁶ The rest seized his servants, mistreated them and killed them."* The deeper meaning here is clear: God has invited us all to be a part of Jesus' future wedding banquet in heaven! Some people declined the coming banquet for the first time. Some have refused many times. Some have gone beyond declining, and when missionaries showed up to tell them about the wedding feast, they literally killed those missionaries.

If you live in the United States, you may not fully understand this because you live in a nation where you are free to be Christian without fear of death, at least currently. Do you realize that approximately 11 people are killed across the globe every day for their faith in Jesus! What happened in this passage is still happening today. Don't take for granted how blessed you are if you live in a nation where you are free to worship God because one day that freedom could be taken from you.

Jesus continued to let them and us know that God does not allow unchecked evil behavior. *⁷ "The king was enraged. He sent his army and destroyed those murderers and burned their city."* To which you might wonder, "why is it acceptable for God to kill those who refuse Him, but not for those who kill God's people?" Does that seem like a double standard? This is a tricky problem in theology, but it isn't just an Old Testament vs. New Testament issue because we see this in both.

Let's take a moment to rewind. In the beginning, we believe God created all life. We believe that God sustains all life. If you disagree with this, you have a bigger problem with understanding who the Creator is and who it is not. God alone appoints a time of death for every person. All people are mortal; some of them die young, and God is responsible for that being allowed to happen. Sometimes God does miracles to keep others alive. Before we ask whether we can trust a God who allowed the death of an innocent person or an evil person, we need to ask whether we can trust a

God who could choose to cut life short for His purpose. Are we okay with the knowledge that God is using death as a tool to turn us into the people He wants us to become? Are we okay knowing that God, who came to earth and died for us, isn't asking us to suffer anything that He hasn't gone through Himself?

God's motivations for death are not the same as those of a human murderer. Most of the time, people kill other people out of hatred or because they want something bad to happen to them or because they don't care about life. God, on the other hand swears to us that this is not why He does it. Ezekiel 33:11 reads: *"As surely as I live, declares the Sovereign Lord, I take no pleasure in the death of the wicked, but rather that they turn from their ways and live."*

In the beginning, God created us and we were free from sin. There was no death and there was perfect unity with God. Mankind brought evil into the world when they chose to sin and not follow God's plan. It is not God who chose death for us. It was our ancestors who condemned us to death by their poor choices, and now by our repeated poor choices. We must understand that every choice affects the generations to come! Make good decisions, if not for your sake, then for the sake of your children.

Jesus was not quite finished: *[8] "Then he said to his servants, 'The wedding banquet is ready, but those I invited did not deserve to come. [9] So go to the street corners and invite to the banquet anyone you find.' [10] So the servants went out into the streets and gathered all the people they could find, the bad as well as the good, and the wedding hall was filled with guests. [11] "But when the king came in to see the guests, he noticed a man there who was not wearing wedding clothes. [12] He asked, 'How did you get in here without wedding clothes, friend?' The man was speechless. [13] "Then the king told the attendants, 'Tie him hand and foot, and throw him outside, into the darkness, where there will be weeping and gnashing of teeth.' [14] "For many are invited, but few are chosen."*

Remember, this is about the kingdom of heaven. Many will be invited; in fact, all are invited to heaven. However, few are chosen. Few will, in fact, make it to heaven. My goal in writing this is to ensure you end up in heaven. The key to ensuring your resting place will be heaven is by having a real, authentic relationship with Jesus. This comes from submitting all of who you are to Jesus and His plans. If you have not done that, there is no better day to do that than today! Here are two questions: **If heaven-bound people produce heavenly fruit on earth, what fruit can you point to that you have produced? If Jesus says many are invited but few enter in, are you sure you are heaven-bound?**

 LIFE APPLICATION

- Performance matters and promises are meaningless. When you look at your Christian life, what can you point to that shows you are performing well for God? Are you giving God the best of your time? The best of your talent? The best of your treasure? Or do you promise you will one day when something in your life changes?
- In today's reading, what did God teach you about God, yourself, and mankind?
- As a result of today's reading, how will you apply what you learned? Answer as, I will…

CHAPTER 66

JESUS' VIEW OF TAXES & ETERNAL MARRIAGE

 Matthew 22:15-33, Mark 12:13-27, Luke 20:20-40

When someone has a viewpoint that is radically different from ours, we tend to try to prove why they are wrong and why we are right. We want to enlighten them as to why their line of thinking is incorrect. You might want to puff up your chest and say, "Not me, I would never do that." However, I doubt it because we all do this at least occasionally. I have seen it in others, and I clearly remember a time or two when I did this myself. That is precisely what you will read about people doing with Jesus.

 Matthew 22:15-22

The Pharisees devised another plan to trick Jesus using the Roman taxation system. Let me explain what happened here: *¹⁶ They sent their disciples to him along with the Herodians.* The religious leaders sent their followers to attempt to trick Jesus. The Pharisees thought Jesus wouldn't pick up on the fact that these people were their disciples. They also sent along these people called Herodians, who supported King Herod's line and agreed to pay taxes to him. The Pharisees objected to paying taxes to Rome. They believed they should only give money to God and not to a government that uses tax dollars for evil. These groups with opposing worldviews were now working together to trap Jesus.

For a Jew, giving money to the temple was a part of everyday life; it was how it had always been. They gave money to the temple, and the temple handled it. That changed when Rome took over their homeland. They had to pay several Roman taxes on top of the temple tax. I imagine no one liked that.

"Teacher," they said, "we know that you are a man of integrity and that you teach the way of God in accordance with the truth. You aren't swayed by others, because you pay no attention to who they are. ¹⁷ Tell us then, what is your opinion? Is it right to pay the imperial tax to Caesar or not?" They finally thought they had trapped Jesus. Just like today, people sweet talk you and then slide the knife in your back when you don't see it coming.

This meant that no matter how Jesus responded to this question, they would have Him trapped! The question would hang Jesus either way because if he said, "Yes, pay them," then He was a traitor to the Jewish cause. He would be answering in favor of the Roman overlords, which would infuriate the Jews. They hated being occupied by a foreign government. Therefore, supporting these taxes would be betraying His own people. On the other hand, if He said, "No, don't pay," He became a revolutionary against Roman rule, and the Romans would take Him out. He was in trouble either way, and that was exactly what they wanted. The Pharisees wanted to ruin His reputation one way or another. It was a lose-lose. Jesus was trapped by their good planning... or so they thought.

¹⁸ But Jesus, knowing their evil intent, said, "You hypocrites, why are you trying to trap me? ¹⁹ Show me the coin used for paying the tax." They brought him a denarius, ²⁰ and he asked them, "Whose image is this? And whose inscription?" ²¹ "Caesar's," they replied. Then he said to them, "So give back to Caesar what is Caesar's, and to God what is God's." Don't miss what Jesus said: don't cheat Caesar, and don't cheat God. This still applies today. Let's be abundantly clear on what Jesus is saying here. He says to pay the taxes your government levies on you, regardless of how you feel about it, and tithe, which means give God 10% of your income. What is odd is that far more people cheat God because the government sees our W2s and would know if we cheated them. On the other hand, there is no tangible consequence to cheating God.

Did you know studies show that the average American gives less than 3% of their income to any charitable cause, including churches? No one in the church knows what you earn, so it is easy to cheat God. The one entity you never want to cheat is God, not the IRS. The IRS might be scary, but they will not be there to double-check your tax returns once Jesus returns. God, however, will be there, asking you what you did with the money He entrusted you with. Here is the point: **Jesus said don't cheat the government and don't cheat God!**

It is also worth noting that it is not your money; it is God's in the first place. He has entrusted you with it for your season of life. Think about what belongs to God because Jesus clearly said, *²¹ "give back to... God what is God's."* Everything belongs to God. Caesar's money even belonged to God. I think Jesus wanted us to linger over the implications of everything belonging to God and the fact that even someone in authority like Caesar was included in that. Everything of yours and mine belongs to God.

Let me show you how we know this. Soon we will see Jesus on trial. Jesus will look at Pilate, and Pilate will say to Him, *"Do you realize that I have power either to free you or authority to crucify you?"* (John 19:10). Jesus replied, *"You would have no power over me if it were not given to you from above"* (John 19:11). Caesar and all of his military might, along with kings, rulers, and presidents of every nation that has existed or is yet to exist, has the authority to rule *only* under the sovereignty of God. I know that is a hard concept for some of us. For an in-depth look at this, read Romans 13. It is all about submitting to the government.

Our submission to any government is shaped by God owning everything. We submit for the Lord's sake. Christians should be humble and submissive, keep the speed limit, obey our parents, submit to our leaders in the church and outside of it, and so on. If we are employees, we should go to work on time, leave on time, and not slack off on what the employer expects. We are people who submit. We do it for the *Lord's* sake.

Therefore, if I render to Caesar the things that are Caesar's, then I give God what is God's because I follow Jesus Christ. I follow His teachings, not my desires, not my spouse's desires, not my culture's teachings. I follow the teachings of Jesus. And then it says, *²² When they heard this, they were amazed. So they left him and went away.*

Many of the teachings of Jesus are very hard to follow. Two thousand years ago, paying taxes was hard because they could barely get by. Today it is hard because we have so much and yet it is never enough. We have different conditions but the same root problem of not having faith in God to provide. The Pharisees failed at trapping Jesus, so now the other ruling religious party was ready to try.

 Matthew 22:23-33

In this passage, the Sadducees present a case, which may sound weird to us, but back then, this practice was more common. There are many stories in the Bible about this practice; read the book of Ruth later to see one such example. The Sadducees asked a great question, one I am sure some of you have wondered about. I will admit that I don't like this teaching from Jesus. I want to be married to Jenny in heaven. I have dated her since 8th grade, and we have been together for the majority of our lives. I literally cannot imagine life without her. However, life is not about what I like or do not like, and I know heaven will be awesome, regardless.

I imagine these Sadducees, upon finishing this story, had a smirk on their faces when asking Jesus their question: *²⁸ "Whose wife would she be in the resurrection?"* Jesus did not shy away from the question for even a moment. He calmly and firmly said they were the ones who strayed from the truth. They were the ones who had been deceived. Now they were showing their ignorance before everyone. They boasted of their superior ability to interpret the Scriptures, and Jesus told them that they did not understand the Scriptures or God. In short, Jesus told them that they had no idea what they were talking about because they did not know the Bible or God. That was a shocking rebuke to these men.

By now, I hope you see that Jesus was often offensive to these men because He told the truth, not what their itching ears wanted to hear. Just because something offends someone does not mean it is not true or should not be said.

The Sadducees had erred because they assumed that life after the resurrection would be the same as it was on earth, including marriage. That belief is still commonly held today. We need to understand that while there will be things that will be as they are now, there is much more that will be different because God will change us.

Studies show that we do not fully utilize our brains. I am confident that when I am able to use 100% of my brain in heaven, I will see things very differently. I know that while it might be hard for me to live with that reality here, I will still submit to God because God is God, and I am not. I trust God with my present and my future.

LIFE APPLICATION

- When taxes are due, we are called to be followers of Jesus who give to the government what is due, and make sure God gets His 10% as well. Honestly evaluate how you are at tithing and giving to God. Not charities, but God. Does He get the first 10% of what He has entrusted you with? If changes need to happen to align your life with the Bible, make them. If not,

rejoice for you are following God's fullness in this area of your life!
- In today's reading, what did God teach you about God, yourself, and mankind?
- As a result of today's reading, how will you apply what you learned? Answer as, I will…

CHAPTER 67

THE GREATEST COMMANDMENT

 Matthew 22:34-46, Mark 12:28-37, Luke 20:41-44

In the last chapter, both the Pharisees' followers and the Sadducees failed at making Jesus look stupid. Now, the other group of religious leaders decided it was their turn: *³⁴ Hearing that Jesus had silenced the Sadducees, the Pharisees got together.* They decided to put their heads together. They thought that they could come up with a plan to take Jesus down for good. The religious leaders were trying to get Jesus to say something that went against what the church taught. They were willfully trying to trap Jesus with theology, and it did not work because little did they know, Jesus wrote all theology. He is the Word of God in full.

We can all get trapped in this mentality. We might not like what a person is saying, so we try to trap them to show everyone why they should not listen to that person. Yet again, this was precisely what these church leaders were trying to do to Jesus. My primary concern is ensuring that we truly understand what Jesus said in His short response. Bear in mind, this is a trap because God gave Moses the Ten Commandments, and He didn't rank them. They were certain they had found a new way to ensnare Jesus.

This passage is also near and dear to my heart because it contains the basis for two-thirds of the mission statement at Family Church, the church I lead. Who would have thought that out of a trap would spring the basis for the purpose of Jesus' people and His future church. Family Church exists to help as many people as possible come to understand how to love God (as defined in the Bible), love people (as defined in the Bible), and make disciples of Jesus who can make more disciples of Jesus (as described in the Bible). You might think the "as defined in the Bible" is not necessary, but it absolutely is! Today, far too many people are trying to redefine what "love" is and who "Jesus" was, is, and always will be.

 Matthew 22:34-46

Let's read this expertly crafted question: *³⁵ One of them, an expert in the law, tested him with this question: ³⁶ "Teacher, which is the greatest commandment in the Law?" ³⁷ Jesus replied: "'Love the Lord your God with all your heart and with all your soul and with all your mind.' ³⁸ This is the first and greatest commandment. ³⁹ And the second is like it: 'Love your neighbor as yourself.' ⁴⁰ All the Law and the Prophets hang on these two commandments."* Do you see it? **Love God and love people.**

Just three sentences from Jesus will take us two chapters to unpack fully. This is the greatest commandment in the Bible. A Pharisee asked Jesus, *³⁶ "Teacher, which is the greatest commandment in the Law?"* Jesus answered in verse 37 by quoting Deuteronomy 6:5. *"'You shall love the Lord your God with all your heart, and with all your soul, and with all your mind.'"* Jesus could have stopped there, but He chose not to.

Remember the question was this: *³⁶ "Which is the greatest commandment in the Law?"* Jesus answered that the greatest and foremost commandment is to fully love God. That is easy to overlook, but so important because before you can even get to the next commandment, you have to embrace this one fully.

What Jesus said next, *³⁹ "'Love your neighbor as yourself'"* comes from the first commandment to first love God. From knowing the overflowing well of God's love, we can then understand how to properly love the entire world. The greatest and most important thing you can do is to love God. Love God with all your heart, soul, mind, and strength. Love God more than your job, spouse, kids, money, house, boat, car, or any other worldly thing. God must come first in all things. Everything begins with a proper understanding and placement of God in our lives.

Jesus said that if you can fully love God and people, then everything in the law and all the things spoken by all the prophets will be accomplished. Everything else in the Old Testament depends on these two things: the commandment to love God and the commandment to love our neighbor. This is an amazing statement. We have the authority of the Son of God telling us something about the origin and design of His entire plan and the Word of God. Here is something overwhelming to ponder: **How can we love other people as much as we love ourselves?**

How in tune with other people do you have to be in order to feel what they feel? How well do you need to know someone before you can long for the same things they do? How deep would your love truly be to say, "I love another person so much that my safety, health, success, and happiness depend on theirs. I feel for that other person as though they **were me**." This sounds and seems impossible... until one day when you have a child.

Growing up, I thought my parents were crazy, just as my kids think I am now. They always told me something I thought was so stupid: "One day you will realize how much I love you." Every time I heard that, I would blow it off and say, "Whatever." Then my first child was born. As soon as I held Addie, I instantly knew what they meant and knew I would do anything to protect and help her. Children open us up to a love that is even deeper than the love for our spouse in many ways.

I believe that kind of love is what Jesus is talking about here but for **all** people, not just your spouse or kids. This is an absolutely staggering commandment. If this is what it means, then something unbelievably powerful, earthshaking, reconstructing, overturning, and upending will have to happen in our souls. Something supernatural. Something well beyond what a self-help book can teach.

Before we apply this to our lives, we must truly grasp the

gravity of what Jesus said. The commandment to love God is the greatest. The commandment to love people as much as we love ourselves is next. He said: *40 "On these two commandments depend the whole Law and the Prophets."* Jesus didn't have to add a third note, but He did. The Pharisee didn't ask this. Jesus went beyond what they asked. He seemed to want to push the importance and centrality of these commandments as much as He could. He said that the commandment to love God is the greatest and foremost. He said the commandment to love your neighbor as you love yourself is *"like it."* That was already more of a detailed response than they had asked for.

Jesus did not simply answer with "love God." Have you ever thought about why He added the second greatest, which He said was like the greatest, to love your neighbor? I believe it is because Jesus wanted us to be stunned at how important these two commandments are. He wanted us to stop and wonder. He wanted us to spend more than a passing moment on these commands and more than a week or two of preaching on the subject at hand. So, he added: *40 "On these two commandments depend the whole Law and the Prophets."*

The Jewish people, by this point in time, had made 613 laws for the people to obey. Jesus was saying scrap those 613 laws because you have all you need to follow if you hold fast to those two commandments. If you are newer to church and you think Jesus was legalistic, like a lot of church people are, He was not! Let's open a window by contrasting what Jesus said here in verse 40 with what He said in Matthew 7:12. (This verse is better known as the Golden Rule or love your neighbor as you love yourself.). *"So in everything, do to others what you would have them do to you, for this sums up the Law and the Prophets."*

This is a profound key to how we can love our neighbor as we love ourselves. God is upholding the Golden Rule by His Fatherly provision. His love for us and our trusting, prayerful love back to

Him is the source of power for living by the Golden Rule. Loving God is invisible. It is an internal and unseen passion of the soul. Loving others is the outward manifestation, the visible expression, the practical demonstration, and, therefore, the fulfillment of what the Old Testament is teaching. **Loving God is made visible by practically and sacrificially loving others.**

The second commandment stands by itself when the New Testament says that love fulfills the law. Romans 13:8-10 is titled, Love of Neighbor Fulfills the Law. *⁸ Let no debt remain outstanding, except the continuing debt to love one another, for whoever loves others has fulfilled the law. ⁹ The commandments, "You shall not commit adultery," "You shall not murder," "You shall not steal," "You shall not covet," and whatever other command there may be, are summed up in this one command: "Love your neighbor as yourself." ¹⁰ Love does no harm to a neighbor. Therefore love is the fulfillment of the law.* Paul says not once but twice that the command to love our neighbor is the *"fulfillment of the law."*

Let's go back to our main passage in Matthew 22. Jesus mentions both love for God and love for neighbor, and He explicitly says in verse 40, *"All the Law and the Prophets hang on these two commandments."* He said something different than what is in the other texts in Matthew 7:12 and Romans 13:8 and 10.

When Jesus said that the Law and the Prophets "hang," He meant that they are dependent on the love of God. God's goal for you, me, and for all of mankind is to love God with a fullness that overflows. He hopes that from that overflow of love that we will express a great love for each other. This means that love is the beginning and the end of why God inspired the Bible. Love is the spring that feeds both ends of the river. Don't miss that! **All of Scripture, all of God's plans, HANG on these two ultimate purposes of life: that we fully love God and that we fully love people.**

If we love God but we do not love other people as much as we love ourselves, we have a religious abuse of power. If you study history, you can sadly see many points in time when the church was more passionate about God than people, and they endorsed some heinous things because of that. That is why God says you cannot leave out either part.

In today's society, our pendulum has swung the other direction, and our culture is all about loving people. The thought now is that if God were real, He would only want me to be happy. Today, life is all about our personal happiness, and the truth of God is pushed to the background. Many churches are siding with culture and saying we should forget or change things God said in the Bible. That is not okay! Jesus said we must have both.

LIFE APPLICATION

- Do you honestly love God more than anything else? Imagine if you and the person who caused you the most strife in life sit down and talk about how loved they feel by you. What would they say? Would they even know you're trying to live out Jesus' commands? Would they laugh at the idea that you are trying to love them as much as you love yourself? Be honest and realign your life where needed.
- In today's reading, what did God teach you about God, yourself, and mankind?
- As a result of today's reading, how will you apply what you learned? Answer as, I will…

_____

_____

_____

_____

CHAPTER 68

GREATEST COMMANDMENT PART II - A SELFLESS COMMAND

 Matthew 22:34-46, Mark 12:28-37, Luke 20:41-44

Being selfless does not come naturally. I have had the privilege of raising four exceptional children. Parenting teaches us a lot about humanity and the corruption that sin has brought into our lives. For example, although I taught my kids to share, it seems that hoarding their favorite toys or food was their built-in response. I never taught my kids to hit their siblings if they did not get their way, but they did so naturally. To be selfish seems to be a default position we are born with. To be selfless is something we must learn in order to become like Jesus.

 Matthew 22:34-46

Jesus' command to ³⁹ *"'Love your neighbor as yourself'"* is an extremely selfless command that cuts to the root of our sinfulness and exposes it. Think about things in your life that you could consider selfish desires. If you cannot think of any, ask your spouse or your kids or a friend. I am confident that the people who really know you could reveal where you are selfish, even if you cannot think of one. The root of our sinfulness is the desire for our happiness, regardless of what God wants and often regardless of what others want. This is important: **All sin comes from a selfish desire to get what we want, regardless of God and others.**

Let's look at the Ten Commandments from Exodus 20 to see how this has always been true and how God has always wanted to help us avoid the pain that self-centeredness causes.

- *Exodus 20:3, You shall have no gods before me & Exodus 20:4-6, Do not worship idols.* Most people would never say they worship idols. An idol is anything that we place before God. It could be our job, kids, spouse, wealth, house, boat, or a man-made object we bow down and worship. When we place other things before God, we are breaking the first two commands out of our selfish desires.
- *Exodus 20:8, Remember the Sabbath day and keep it holy.* Why don't most people set aside one FULL day to honor God and rest? The answer is simple in that we think we have too much to do. Could part of the reason we are always worn out stem from the fact that we do not rest like God calls us to because we selfishly think His plan is not good?
- *Exodus 20:12, Honor thy father and mother.* We don't do that because of selfish desire. Throughout most of our lives we think that we know better or believe we have better plans than our parents do.
- *Exodus 20:13, You shall not murder.* Most of us wouldn't do that. However, those who have murdered did it because they lost control and cared less about the person than their selfish desires.
- *Exodus 20:14, You shall not commit adultery.* People do this when they think life will be better with someone else other than their spouse. The choice to pursue this idea is driven from selfish desires.
- *Exodus 20:15, You shall not steal, :16, give false testimony, or :17, covet.* Again, we selfishly do these things because we want what others have or want to protect ourselves.

Each sin-filled action results from our desire to get what we want, regardless of what God says or how it affects others. This command of Jesus cuts to the root of sin, exposes it, and tells us how to sever its power over us. Jesus understood the inborn, deep, defining human trait of our love for ourselves. Children are not taught how to say "mine." Parents don't teach children to hit their brother or sister—it naturally happens when they don't get what they want. What a child wants, they take, or they fight for it. Everyone, without exception, has this human trait. Culture doesn't have to teach us to stop listening to our parents; we do it naturally when we don't get our way.

I will be honest. I thought my parents were so out of touch when I was growing up. Now that I am a parent, I realize how right they were. I'm in the season of life where my kids think I am out of touch; that is how it works. We all have a powerful instinct for self-preservation and self-fullfillment.

When Jesus said, [39] *"as yourself,"* He meant that He wants us to desire the best for others as much as we do for ourselves. To hunger for food is not evil. To want to be warm in the winter is not evil. To want to be safe or to be healthy during a plague is not evil. To want your life to count in some significant way is not evil. To desire things is not evil within itself. Whether it has become evil in your life will be exposed as you hear and respond to Jesus' commandment. Jesus said, "As you love, as you care for, as you treat yourself, do the same for your neighbor."

This means that when you desire food, you also desire to feed your neighbor. As you long for nice clothes for yourself, long for nice clothes for others. As you work and live in a comfortable place, you desire a comfortable place for those who are homeless. As you seek to be safe and secure from calamity or violence, seek help from those who have gone through it. As you seek friends for yourself, be a friend to those without. As you want your life to count and be significant, help others find their God-given purpose. **Life should be about serving God first, and then serving others as much as you serve your interests.**

[39] *"'Love your neighbor as yourself.'"* Circle that word "as." Underline "as." Jesus didn't say, "similarly or like," He said "as."

³⁹ "'Love your neighbor as yourself.'" Don't only say you want to help others; act on that desire! Jesus was not just saying to seek for your neighbor the *same things* you seek for yourself, but to seek them in the *same way,* with the same zeal, passion, energy, creativity, and so on. Think about this. How do you pursue your own happiness? Now contrast that to how you pursue the happiness of your neighbor or co-worker? If you are honest, doing what Jesus is asking seems overwhelming.

I think Jesus wanted us to feel that tension because it makes us lean into the source that is beyond us: God. This forces us to fully love God first, and then we are able to love others this way secondly. It's the first commandment that makes the second commandment doable. *³⁷ "'Love the Lord your God with all your heart and with all your soul and with all your mind'"* is the basis of the second commandment, which is a visible expression of the first.

"Love... God with all your heart" **means that you place God first in all things.**

"Love... God... with all your soul" **means that God defines your true purpose.**

"Love... God... with all your mind" **means that God's Word guides your decisions.**

In other words, take all your self-focus and all your longing for joy, hope, love, security, fulfillment, and significance and focus it on God. Once you do that, He will fully satisfy your heart, soul, and mind. There, you will find fulfillment and transformation that makes the second commandment possible. Once you do that,

39 **"*'Love your neighbor as yourself.'*"** That is how we can get to the place where we can say, "Oh, yes, I love myself. I have longings for joy and satisfaction and fulfillment and significance and security. But after all God has done for me, I cannot wait to help others find those same things I desire through Him!"

I promise you, if you seek God like this one day, you will be able to find as much joy in giving someone in need a coat as buying a new coat for yourself. That may sound impossible to some of you, but it is not! I promise that if you seek God like this one day, even when something is going bad in your life, you will still be a joyful person because your source of joy will no longer come from your circumstances.

Loving your neighbor does not threaten your love of self because self-love has become God-love, and God-love is not threatened, diminished, or exhausted by being poured into the lives of others. There will be hard choices about what to give up and what to keep. There will be different interpretations of what is good for another person. It is important to remember that even when we face a fork in the road, His grace is always sufficient. When we love others out of the overflow of our love for God, we will make the best decisions.

This is a pivotal command, and that is why we parked here for two chapters. This command cuts to the root of sin and our selfish desire for self-fulfillment. In the first commandment, God focuses the passion to be firmly happy in God and God alone. In the second commandment, God opens a whole world of being a joyful conduit from God to other people. Human beings, everywhere you find them, are designed to receive and enlarge your joy in God. Love people the way you love yourself. Show them and give them—through every practical means available—what you have found for yourself in God.

 LIFE APPLICATION

- Can you describe your life as a conduit of love and joy? Is your life filled with such love and joy from God that it naturally overflows into other people? Be honest and realign your life where necessary. If you need to spend more time with God to be filled with Him, start realigning your time. If you're filled with God but love is not flowing to others, find a way to give away more of yourself to others.
- In today's reading, what did God teach you about God, yourself, and mankind?
- As a result of today's reading, how will you apply what you learned? Answer as, I will…

CHAPTER 69

LEARNING FROM HYPOCRITES

 Matthew 23

In the previous chapters, Jesus addressed several sensitive topics when the religious leaders asked questions to trap Him in a theological conundrum. However, the traps backfired when Jesus blew them away with His answers. The people who opposed Jesus realized they were not going to win their verbal sparring matches with Jesus. They were not going to be able to trap Him with theology or discredit Him. It would appear that they gave up, but soon you will see they just devised a new tactical approach.

Most people know that when a person or group opposes something, they will mercilessly and unceasingly try every tactic to destroy their opposition until they receive what they want. American politics and ancient politics are similar. The tactics the religious leaders used in Jesus' time will be similar to what we see in our culture today. Read Jesus' conversation with His followers about the same religious leaders. Be prepared. Jesus does not beat around the bush.

 Matthew 23:1-39

That passage stings a bit. Remember that as Jesus taught this lesson, He was at the Jewish temple. This meant many religious leaders were sitting around Him. These leaders listened to every single woe from Jesus. Jesus used strong and clear language. Imagine if a preacher said that about the people in his church! It wouldn't go any better today than it did then. However, we can learn from this if we drop our defensive reactions. God included this passage for a reason. One takeaway is this: **Choose to be open to learning how all Scripture applies to your life.**

The definition of a hypocrite is a person who pretends to have certain beliefs, attitudes, or feelings when they really do not. An example of a hypocrite is someone who says they care about the environment but are constantly littering. Here is a weird fact about me: I minored in theatre, and the word "hypocrite" originates from the theatre. It dates back to when actors wore a variety of masks to pretend to be someone different and even someone they had no intention of ever becoming in real life.

This passage reminds me of the two times we saw Jesus become so angry with the religious leaders that He drove them out of the temple. Those two instances, and this one, contain the harshest words Jesus ever used to convey His point. He called them hypocrites seven times! Five times He called them blind guides. Twice, He called them fools. He capped it off by calling them serpents and a brood of vipers! Despite such strong condemnation, we can make a choice to learn from hypocrites.

In this passage, we find three main issues that Jesus took them to task for.

Issue One: These teachers of the law were failures in teaching truth.

[13] "Woe to you, teachers of the law and Pharisees, you hypocrites! You shut the door of the kingdom of heaven in people's faces. You yourselves do not enter, nor will you let those enter who are trying to. [14] [15] "Woe to you, teachers of the law and Pharisees, you hypocrites! You travel over land and sea to win a single convert, and when you have succeeded, you make them twice as much a child of hell as you are."

Their teaching was failing to save others. They failed to show others the way to the kingdom of heaven. Jesus told the religious leaders they would not be going to heaven. The whole point of being a spiritual leader was to lead people closer to God, not further from Him. While no pastor or leader would ever say their goal is to lead people away from God, we need to be careful in what we do and what we teach, or we could end up in this same position.

Their teaching was also leading people to be worse. They were not teaching them to become more like God but to be more like Satan or the enemy of God. Perhaps this happened because they placed emphasis on the traditions of men rather than on living out the Word of God.

Remember, the Pharisees knew the Bible well. The best Pharisees memorized the entire first five books of the Old Testament, but they did not allow it to transform their lives. They neglected God's word and starved those who received their teaching. We must be careful not to put ourselves, or our favorite traditions, between God's word and those we teach. Instead we must let them know *"the whole will of God"* (Acts 20:27). If our traditions come between people knowing Jesus, we need to abolish our traditions.

Their teaching was making distinctions where God did not. *16 "Woe to you, blind guides! You say, 'If anyone swears by the temple, it means nothing; but anyone who swears by the gold of the temple is bound by that oath.' 17 You blind fools! Which is greater: the gold, or the temple that makes the gold sacred? 18 You also say, 'If anyone swears by the altar, it means nothing; but anyone who swears by the gift on the altar is bound by that oath.' 19 You blind men! Which is greater: the gift, or the altar that makes the gift sacred? 20 Therefore, anyone who swears by the altar swears by it and by everything on it. 21 And anyone who swears by the temple swears by it and by the one who dwells in it. 22 And anyone who swears by heaven swears by God's throne and by the one who sits on it."*

The scribes and Pharisees made fine distinctions between the types of oaths one could swear. We can easily do similar things today, such as holding up some of God's commands as essential to salvation while ignoring others because we don't like them. We can also teach our thoughts and opinions rather than sharing what the Bible says and leaving it at that. Our thoughts and opinions are never equal to God's.

Jesus took the leaders to task for the next issue, **being inconsistent in practice,** which is so easy for us to fall into. *23 "Woe to you, teachers of the law and Pharisees, you hypocrites! You give a tenth of your spices—mint, dill and cumin. But you have neglected the more important matters of the law—justice, mercy and faithfulness. You should have practiced the latter, without neglecting the former."*

They were **neglecting the commands of God.** Truthfully, we all struggle with this. No one perfectly follows all of God's directions in life. Jesus made it clear that tithing or giving God 10% of your earnings was great, but it doesn't stop a person from neglecting other equally important things. We should never strive to neglect anything God commands us to do. The religious leaders' problem was that they were not willing to admit where they fell short, and they pretended to be something they were not—a hypocrite.

Today, many Christians have this neglectful giving in reverse. Most Christians no longer tithe or give 10% back to God. Many of them do good things—they love justice and mercy—but Jesus clearly said the key is to do all of it, not just what you prefer.

Let me expand on why I think it has shifted today. In Jesus' time, people saw your tithe. They saw the amount of food you brought into the temple to offer or the animals you gave. The tithe was meant to be seen, and the people made sure to tithe so everyone could see how good they were. However, they neglected other things. Since it was not as easy to see, they didn't do it.

Today, social justice is a big agenda item. Everyone can see what you stand for based on the marches you attend. It is very public, so people are all about it and want everyone to know what they stand for. On the other hand, today no one knows what you tithe because it is done more privately. So, it makes sense why the social scales have flipped. This leads into another point by Jesus.

Issue Two: Consistent practice of the holy things of God had been replaced with an outward focus on elevating self.

[25] "Woe to you, teachers of the law and Pharisees, you hypocrites! You clean the outside of the cup and dish, but inside they are full of greed and self-indulgence. [26] Blind Pharisee! First clean the inside of the cup and dish, and then the outside also will be clean. [27] "Woe to you, teachers of the law and Pharisees, you hypocrites! You are like whitewashed tombs, which look beautiful on the outside but on the inside are full of the bones of the dead and everything unclean. [28] In the same way, on the outside you appear to people as righteous but on the inside you are full of hypocrisy and wickedness."

The leaders were far more concerned with keeping traditions and showing off rather than striving to be godly. They were willing to look past all kinds of hidden sin. We also struggle with this. We can be guilty of having the wrong focus. We can focus more on our career than our relationship with Jesus. As a church, we can focus more on the size of crowds rather than on how many people we can truly share the good news of Jesus with. It is easy for us to attend church and pretend to be perfect on the outside but be broken on the inside. As a culture, we want to pretend everything is going great, even when our marriage is falling apart or we lose our job. Jesus clearly said that acting that was not okay.

Issue Three: They were honoring the past but were unwilling to live like it.

²⁹ "Woe to you, teachers of the law and Pharisees, you hypocrites! You build tombs for the prophets and decorate the graves of the righteous. ³⁰ And you say, 'If we had lived in the days of our ancestors, we would not have taken part with them in shedding the blood of the prophets.' ³¹ So you testify against yourselves that you are the descendants of those who murdered the prophets." They pretended that they would not have acted like their ancestors if they had lived in the past. They believed that they would have been better people. The ironic part to me was that they said they would never murder prophets like their ancestors did, yet soon they would do that exact thing to Jesus.

Jesus finished with this: *³² "Go ahead, then, and complete what your ancestors started! ³³ "You snakes! You brood of vipers! How will you escape being condemned to hell? ³⁴ Therefore I am sending you prophets and sages and teachers. Some of them you will kill and crucify; others you will flog in your synagogues and pursue from town to town. ³⁵ And so upon you will come all the righteous blood that has been shed on earth, from the blood of righteous Abel to the blood of Zechariah son of Berekiah, whom you murdered between the temple and the altar. ³⁶ Truly I tell you, all this will come on this generation ³⁷ "Jerusalem, Jerusalem, you who kill the prophets and stone those sent to you, how often I have longed to gather your children together, as a hen gathers her chicks under her wings, and you were not willing. ³⁸ Look, your house is left to you desolate. ³⁹ For I tell you, you will not see me again until you say, 'Blessed is he who comes in the name of the Lord.'"* I wonder how most would answer the following question: **Will I be like the Pharisees and refuse to live out what I say I believe?**

That question is the essence of the problem. Some who grew up in the modern church, know right from wrong, study

Scripture, attend Bible studies, and talk like they are followers of God; yet, they do not allow any of their knowledge to change their lives. They do not let their knowledge of right and wrong define how they live, nor do they allow their understanding of the Bible to change how they operate. Just like the Pharisees, they outwardly talk the talk, but inwardly, they are hypocrites. **Are you a Christian actor or are you a genuine Christian?**

 LIFE APPLICATION

- Jesus was not a fan of hypocrites. Are there areas where you know you are not living up to what Jesus wants for you? Don't be like the religious leaders of Jesus' day who knew the truth and yet did nothing to change.
- In today's reading, what did God teach you about God, yourself, and mankind?
- As a result of today's reading, how will you apply what you learned? Answer as, I will…

CHAPTER 70

JESUS ON END TIMES – PART 1

 Matthew 24

I told you in book two of this series that my papa wasn't a believer until right before he died. I think a little more of his story fits well right here.

My papa grew up in an abusive home, lied about his age to join the Navy at 16, and was shooting down enemy planes as a gunner shortly thereafter. He saw a lot of stuff that convinced him there wasn't a God, or if there was, He was a mean God. The only two people he loved growing up were his Grandpa George and his Grandpa Charlie. One of them taught him that ending up in heaven or hell was based on what you made of life here on earth.

Papa was a good and moral man. He strived to be honest and truthful, but he observed many church-going people who were hypocrites. He knew far too many churchgoers who were holy on Sunday but were cheats, philanderers, gossips, or otherwise awful people for the remainder of the week. Papa didn't like that, and so he decided he didn't need their God. Jesus was also opposed to people saying one thing and doing something else. Keep this in mind as we read Matthew 24.

 Matthew 24:1-14

When I originally preached this chapter as a sermon, it was a strange timing because it was the week after churches were forced to close because of COVID. In Michigan, the big three auto manufacturers closed down, many business leaders laid people off, and people were scared. Several people asked me if this was the end times the Bible talked about. They wondered if this was when the Anti-Christ would rise because our world was ending. I had people send me conspiracy theories one after the other. I sat back and said to God, "Your timing is amazing." It was perfect timing because as many people began to think that this could be the end of time for all of us, I began writing this as a sermon.

Chapter 24 occurred right after Jesus left the temple for the last time. He told His followers what would happen in the years ahead. *¹ Jesus left the temple and was walking away when his disciples came up to him to call his attention to its buildings. ² "Do you see all these things?" he asked. "Truly I tell you, not one stone here will be left on another; every one will be thrown down."*

Imagine being Jesus' followers. You just left this very temple that He references and you know it is the center of Jewish life and worship. The temple was the most sacred place for these people; it was God's place. Jesus was just there teaching. Now Jesus was telling them this whole place would be destroyed and that not one stone would be left unturned. Clearly, they would have been wondering how that was possible. They would have thought that Rome would never let that happen in such an important city. Surely the Jewish leaders wouldn't let that happen, and most certainly God wouldn't either!

The cool part about history is that it tells us whether what Jesus said was true or false. If Jesus had said this and it had not happened, there would be no point in following Him or listening to Him. Study history and you will find that in 70 A.D., the Jewish people revolted against Rome. Rome didn't respond kindly to opposition. Emperor Titus made them pay for trying to revolt by destroying Jewish people and their precious temple. We know it was demolished because the golden walls and roof melted in the fire. The Roman army had to dig the gold out of the foundation to take it to Titus. I hope you see that the Bible is far more than a random fairy tale but instead is based on real human history.

³ As Jesus was sitting on the Mount of Olives, the disciples came to him privately. "Tell us," they said, "when will this happen, and what will be the sign of your coming and of the end of the age?" ⁴ Jesus answered: "Watch out that no one deceives you. ⁵ For many will come in my name, claiming, 'I am the Messiah,' and will deceive many. ⁶ You will hear of wars and rumors of wars, but see to it that you are not alarmed. Such things must happen, but the end is still to come. ⁷ Nation will rise against nation, and kingdom against kingdom. There will be famines and earthquakes in various places. ⁸ All these are the beginning of birth pains."

Jesus said this would happen and indeed it did. However, we need to read supporting documents outside of the Bible. The Jewish historian Josephus documented every one of these things when they happened, again, proving the Bible is 100% accurate.

Jesus continued with a pep talk for His disciples. Let's read this inspirational speech: *⁹ "Then you will be handed over to be persecuted and put to death, and you will be hated by all nations because of me. ¹⁰ At that time many will turn away from the faith and will betray and hate each other, ¹¹ and many false prophets will appear and deceive many people. ¹² Because of the increase of wickedness, the love of most will grow cold, ¹³ but the one who stands firm to the end will be saved."*

I can't imagine the disciples saying, "Sweet, sign me up for that!" Imagine if I said, "I have an amazing volunteer opportunity for you, but it is going to lead to you being persecuted, hated by everyone, and then put to death." Would you sign up? I honestly doubt it.

The end of this passage is key—phrasing matters. Jesus does not say multitudes, nor the many. He said, *¹³ "the one..."* Why would Jesus phrase it as one, not many, not multitudes? Why one?

The truth is, following Jesus is not easy. No hands will ever fly into the air, anxious to volunteer to be hated, persecuted, and killed. Having to battle false teachers and constant betrayal is brutal. It is hard to follow the straight and very narrow path. *¹³ "But the one who stands firm to the end will be saved."*

If we are honest, we would prefer if Jesus had said, "But the one who stands for Me sometimes, or most of the time, or until it gets hard, they will all be saved." However, that was not what Jesus said. **Jesus said it takes standing firm, no matter what life throws at you, to the very end of life… that is what it takes to live a faithful life.**

That is sobering.

Let's keep reading because this next part is where Jesus talked more clearly about the end times. *¹⁴ "And this gospel of the kingdom will be preached in the whole world as a testimony to all nations, and then the end will come."*

There are differing statistics, but it is estimated that about 40% of our world has never been reached with the Good News of Jesus. He said He will not return until His Gospel has been preached to the whole world. If you really want Jesus to come soon, receive training to reach the unreached people groups!

Matthew 24:15-50

Biblical scholars point out that in 167 B.C., Antiochus fulfilled the prophecy we just read. He invaded Jerusalem, captured the city, marched into the Temple Mount, erected a statue of Zeus, and sacrificed a pig on the Jewish altar of incense. It's interesting how history and the Bible tie together so well. Jesus warned the disciples that times would be hard. People would try to say it was the end, and people would claim to be the messiah who returned, but Jesus said, "Do not follow them!" Jesus said it would be evident to everyone when He returned, so don't be deceived!

If you are not aware, there have been men all over the world who have claimed to be Jesus. When I was in the Philippines, I heard about some large churches throughout the country whose founder claimed to be Jesus. The church grew like crazy, but then the unthinkable happened—the founder died. When I was there, the son of the now-dead founder, proclaimed he was Jesus. While we think that sounds crazy, people fall for all kinds of false teachings.

In verses 30-31, most of us get the picture of Jesus' return up in the clouds. People seemingly fly up to meet Him in the sky. In verse 32 is where the *Left Behind* series came from, which was popular years ago.

What was the name Jesus gave to the religious leaders in our last chapter? Hypocrites. Do you think it is a coincidence that He used that word in this explanation? I don't think so. Jesus wanted to ensure we knew that living a fake life for Him would not result in our destination being heaven. Jesus always engages with us and instructs us on how to reflect what we believe. Jesus has never been excited when we choose to go to a church one day a week but live like the world the rest of the week.

[14] "And this gospel of the kingdom will be preached in the whole world as a testimony to all nations, and then the end will come. where there will be weeping and gnashing of teeth..."

There is so much we can unpack and teach here, and there are many theories about what this means. A vast array of perspectives and entire church doctrines have been built around the end times. Most of us know someone who is into end times theology and what it all means. What I want us all to focus on has nothing to do with how the rapture works or when Christians might be taken to heaven or how long Christians might have to suffer. What we need to focus on has nothing to do with the theories but simply what Jesus asked us to focus on. It is so easy to get sidetracked and focused on things that don't really matter.

If you boil it down to what matters for all people, then and today, it is simple—**be prepared**. Focus on being prepared for His return. Make sure you are always living for Him. Honestly, that is hard because when something tough happens, we rarely want to act like Jesus! But that is what we are called to do. The key here is this: **It is critical to always strive to be like Jesus.** It is critical to be prepared and not wait until we are about to die to get right with God. That is what Jesus was saying.

No one knows when Jesus will return, and you do not want to be on the wrong side when He does. I know there are some who grew up thinking, or currently think, that God is in heaven waiting for you to make a mistake to catch you. You live in fear of making a mistake because you are sure Jesus will come back as soon as you do. That is not how God operates! I can say this with assurance because that is not how we as parents operate with our children. We don't wait in the shadows for our kids to make a mistake so we can pounce on them. The Bible says if we, who are sinful people, know how to give good things to our children, then God, who is sinless and perfect, will do far better. God loves you, and the reason He wants to keep you living a godly life is not to hurt you but to protect you from hurt.

Following God's direction in life will save many people from so much pain. The problem is we choose to ignore God, and then we end up in pain that could have been avoided.

Can we go back to the story of my grandfather when he was young? He desperately needed to see Jesus in those around him. He didn't, and so by default he ignored Jesus. It took him until his deathbed to finally realize a few Christians did live what they said they believed and that not all of them were hypocrites. The lost are watching you and looking for a reason to believe in or reject Jesus. Listen to Jesus and live a life where, at any moment, you are ready to see Jesus while others see Jesus through you. I promise that if you do, it will be a much better life than always looking over your shoulder and wondering or being riddled with guilt.

 **LIFE APPLICATION**

- Are you prepared if Jesus returned today? Are you living a "holy" life? If not, what steps should you take to be more prepared starting today?
- In today's reading, what did God teach you about God, yourself, and mankind?
- As a result of today's reading, how will you apply what you learned? Answer as, I will…

CHAPTER 71

JESUS ON END TIMES – PART 2

 Matthew 25

The passage you are going to read is not a story about a bunch of young women about to get married. This was a story about several people who thought they were followers of God. Some of you may define yourself as a follower of God, but some of you reading this are still checking out this Jesus thing, and I am so glad you are.

Matthew 25:1-5 tells us that all ten women were there waiting for the bridegroom, who was late. However, only five of them had put in the effort to ensure they were prepared by having the extra oil needed to keep their lamps burning. Five planned more, prepared more, and thought through the long-term implications of their choices. The others chose to roll with it and decided that their normal amount of effort would suffice. Unfortunately, they ran out of oil and could not rely on the others to give them any.

This sounds like so many of us in life. There are those who prefer to do as little as possible to get by and others who love to put in extra effort. That is the reality of the uniqueness of people. Some of us do as little as possible at our jobs, while others go above and beyond. Some of us read our Bibles occasionally, while others dig deeper and study more. Some of us do only what our coaches make us do to prepare for games, while others work out and practice outside of scheduled times. Everyone knows that the person who puts in more effort is far more likely to be successful than the person who puts in the bare minimum. Like the parable, we are each responsible for having our own personal relationship with Jesus and for trusting fully in Him for everything. We cannot be like the five who were unprepared and only rely on the faith of another person (such as a parent or spouse) to get us into heaven.

📖 Matthew 25:1-13

In verse one, you read that all the women knew that the bridegroom was coming at some point in the future, and they were waiting. What separated them was that Jesus did not know five of them, *¹² "But he replied, 'Truly I tell you, I don't know you.'"* It did not matter that if they knew Jesus. It did not matter if they knew where to be, how to dress, or how to talk. Jesus said they could not come in because **He did not know them.** Here is the point: **Real followers of Jesus know Jesus and are known by Jesus.**

You can spend your entire life in church and know a lot about Jesus but not have a relationship with Him or be known by Him. In chapter 53, we learned that Jesus said the religious leaders were not destined for heaven because they were faking it. If you are reading this and you have been faking your relationship with Jesus, you know it. You know that you do not read your Bible. You know you do not pray and seek Jesus. You know it is just a show. If that is you, I beg you, listen to Jesus! Jesus said if He does not **know you,** the door will be closed! My goal is that none of you hear those words come from His mouth. My goal is to build real, fully devoted followers of Jesus Christ who will make other fully devoted followers of Jesus Christ.

 Matthew 25:14-30

That is my kind of boss! Who wouldn't love to have a bag of gold handed to them, let alone five bags of gold! Another way to refer to one bag of gold is one talent, which was worth about twenty years of a day laborer's wage. To put this into context, the boss handed one laborer twenty years' worth of wages! To another, he handed a lifetime of wages! He handed another worker enough to support him, his wife, and their children for life! That is incredible, but in verse 15 we see that each was given different amounts *"according to his ability."*

God does not give us all the same gifts and talents. God is not a socialist when it comes to money, gifts, or talents. Our cultural worldview is all about everyone being equal and the same. It is important to understand that is not a Biblical worldview. This means that as Christians, we acknowledge that God creates every person differently, and that is a good thing. God gifts us all in unique ways, and that is His perfect plan.

I'm confident that those of you who have been in church for a long time know the phrase we all hope to hear God say to us some day. It is not a coincidence that we see it here. *²¹ 'Well done, good and faithful servant! You have been faithful with a few things; I will put you in charge of many things. Come and share your master's happiness!'* However, those who choose another path will hear a different message like the women did earlier in this chapter. My prayer is that none of you hear God say, *³⁰ 'And throw that worthless servant outside, into the darkness, where there will be weeping and gnashing of teeth.'*

This is a great ending to a great story for the faithful. It is not a happy story for the one who did nothing. Those who had fake faith, those people were destined for a very different place: hell. The main point Jesus communicated is this: **Being ready for His return demands service to Him that produces fruit.**

I know some who have been in church for a long time are thinking we are saved by grace alone. That is 100% true. If salvation was just about getting to heaven, wouldn't we teleport to heaven as soon as we are saved? Why are we left on earth? Why does God leave us here if not to DO the work of leading other people to Jesus? There is no place in the Bible where Jesus said to relax and do nothing. He never says to not talk to people about Him if you are scared, to only go to church one day a week and then live for yourself. The key point: **Your life was designed**

by God to be invest *in* others. Please don't wait until it is too late.

 Matthew 25:31-46

The time will come when God will separate all people. They will be separated based on those who followed Him and those who did not. *³⁴ "Then the King will say to those on his right, 'Come, you who are blessed by my Father; take your inheritance, the kingdom prepared for you since the creation of the world. Some will be invited into heaven! Invited into the presence of God! Why only some? ³⁵ For I was hungry and you gave me something to eat, I was thirsty and you gave me something to drink, I was a stranger and you invited me in, ³⁶ I needed clothes and you clothed me, I was sick and you looked after me, I was in prison and you came to visit me.'"* They were not invited in because they said a prayer as a kid or were baptized as a kid or warmed up a seat in church every Sunday. They were invited in because they accepted Jesus as their Savior and then lived *like* Him!

The followers' response is stunning. *³⁷ "Then the righteous will answer him, 'Lord, when did we see you hungry and feed you, or thirsty and give you something to drink? ³⁸ When did we see you a stranger and invite you in, or needing clothes and clothe you? ³⁹ When did we see you sick or in prison and go to visit you?'"* They don't remember doing this for Jesus! This was simply the lifestyle they chose in living for their King. They truly loved Jesus, so they lived like Jesus. They were generous people and had no idea that they were serving Jesus by serving others.

Jesus replied, *⁴⁰ "The King will reply, 'Truly I tell you, whatever you did for one of the least of these brothers and sisters of mine, you did for me.'"* Jesus became such a part of who they were as faithful followers of God that they cared for people. Jesus said, when you took care of those people, brought a meal to your neighbor in need, drove him to the doctor, picked up a few things at the store for her, or sent that homebound person a card, you were taking care of Jesus, your King! Wow, that is awesome!

How are you doing at that? How are you caring for other people? How are you loving other people? How are you doing at not overlooking people in need around you? Jesus clearly says that is crucial... and it is about to get even more important.

⁴¹ "Then he will say to those on his left, 'Depart from me, you who are cursed, into the eternal fire prepared for the devil and his angels. ⁴² For I was hungry and you gave me nothing to eat, I was thirsty and you gave me nothing to drink, ⁴³ I was a stranger and you did not invite me in, I needed clothes and you did not clothe me, I was sick and in prison and you did not look after me.'" I find it strange that they mirrored the last group with their response. *⁴⁴ "They also will answer, 'Lord, when did we see you hungry or thirsty or a stranger or needing clothes or sick or in prison, and did not help you?' ⁴⁵ "He will reply, 'Truly I tell you, whatever you did not do for one of the least of these, you did not do for me.' ⁴⁶ "Then they will go away to eternal punishment, but the righteous to eternal life."*

The response is the same but in the opposite direction. Jesus said, "When you are choosing not to be My disciple and follower and are only focusing on yourself rather than those in need around you, then you are choosing to live a lifestyle separate from Me."

That is hard teaching and a harsh reality. Let me encourage you to be a true follower of Jesus who freely helps, serves, and leads other people toward Him. Make your goal to help as many people as possible reach heaven. That is why these books were created, to help you come to know the real Jesus and share Him with as many people as possible. Be a disciple of Jesus who makes more disciples of Jesus.

 **LIFE APPLICATION**

- If Jesus returned today, are you prepared? Are you living a "holy" life? What steps should you take to be more prepared starting today?
- In today's reading, what did God teach you about God, yourself, and mankind?
- As a result of today's reading, how will you apply what you learned? Answer as, I will…

FROM PASTOR ADAM

Congratulations on finishing the third book in *The Real Jesus* series! I hope that as you continue to learn about Jesus, you are applying His life-transforming teachings in your life. I hope that you are actively guiding others through these books and helping those you have guided through the books do the same with others. If you need help becoming a disciple of Jesus, or if you want to learn how to make more disciples of Jesus, please email us at dm@familychurch.app, and we will be glad to assist you in any way we can. We can even partner you with someone to help you walk through these books virtually or in person and teach you how to do the same with others!

NEXT IN *THE REAL JESUS* SERIES

Grab a copy of Book 4 in *The Real Jesus* series so you can continue learning, growing, and making disciples of Jesus! In the final book, you will learn why you don't need to worry, how to find joy when life isn't perfect, how Jesus was betrayed, and how Jesus died. You will then read stories about all the people who saw Jesus resurrected after His death, and so much more!

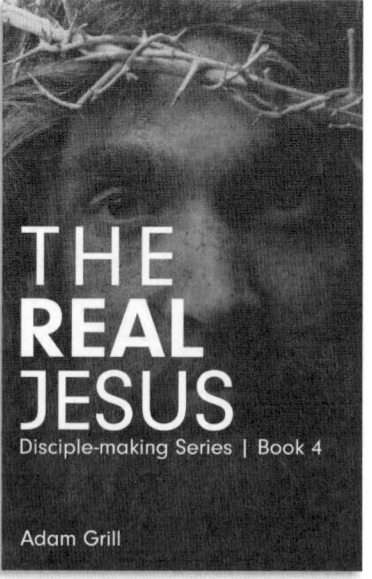

Also available in *The Real Jesus* Disciple-making Series:

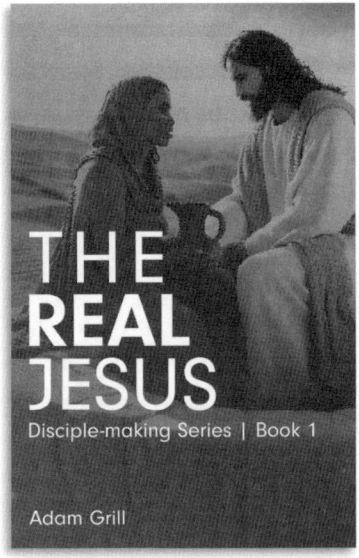

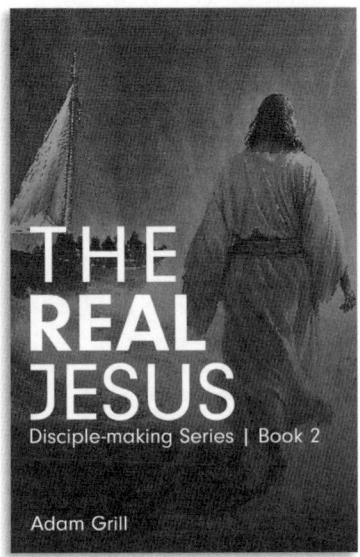

Find more disciple-making tools here!

NOTES